Life Is A Gift

Sixty Years of Medical Practice

EDWIN PARKER, M. D.

LOST COAST PRESS

Life is a Gift: Sixty Years of Medical Practice

Lost Coast Press
155 Cypress Street
Fort Bragg, CA 95437
(800) 773-7782
www.cypresshouse.com

Book design and production: Cypress House
Cover design: Chuck Hathaway / Mendocino Graphics

Library of Congress Cataloging-in-Publication Data

Parker, Edwin, 1917-
Life is a gift : sixty years of medical practice / Edwin Parker.
p. cm.
Includes bibliographical references and index.
ISBN 1-882897-76-5 (pbk.)
1. Parker, Edwin, 1917- 2. Physicians--United States--Biography. I. Title.
R154.P2517A3 2003
610'.92—dc21 2003001785

Printed in Canada

2 4 6 8 9 7 5 3 1

Acknowledgements

I am thankful to many: to my wife, Mable, for her kindness, patience, and help; to my daughter, Judy, and my son, Geoffrey, for their untiring composure, and the effort they made in typing and retyping the many changes I made as I plodded along; to Bill Bockus, a good and true friend who inspired, persisted, and pushed me into writing this book from beginning to end. I am also grateful to the Great Spirit, whose voice I hear in the winds: thanks for listening and reminding me to keep this work simple, clear, and true.

Contents

Foreword

Edwin Parker, M.D., F.A.C.O.G., retired in the year 2000 after practicing medicine for over sixty years. His specialty was obstetrics and gynecology. He graduated from St. Louis University Medical School in June 1940. This was followed by one year of internship and one year of residency in surgery and obstetrics in Cleveland, Ohio.

On December 7, 1941, during his residency, the Japanese bombed Pearl Harbor. Dr. Parker volunteered for the army immediately, but was not called for service until October 1942. He spent three years in the armed services during World War II, which included training in the medical battalion of General Patton's 6th Armored Division in the desert of Rice, California. While there he was transferred to New Britain, a 300-mile-long island off the northeast coast of New Guinea in the South Pacific. He was promptly assigned to an evacuation hospital where the need for surgeons was sudden and acute. The Japanese Air Force had just bombed this hospital in broad daylight, killing more than half of its medical staff and injuring most other doctors and patients. At that time the entire 300-bed hospital was quartered in tents in an open field. Atop each tent was displayed a huge red cross—it was a target you could not miss from the air.

The very next day after the attack, the Army Corp of Engineers began bulldozing trenches, long, deep, narrow excavations in the ground that looked like spokes on a wheel. On its hub were the operating rooms. All was covered with large, long palm trunks and many layers of sandbags. Atop, they were camouflaged with nets and foliage, so that the hospital was no longer a visible target from above.

The Japanese had captured Rabaul, which lies on the northern tip of New Britain, in 1942. They stationed most of their naval vessels and a good part of their air force there until 1945. The evacuation hospital was located a little over 100 miles south of Rabaul.

Dr. Parker was most reluctant about my mentioning his war record. He insisted this book was not his autobiography, and saw no reason to discuss it. I, however, feel it helps to know all you can about an author, his life, and his thoughts, so I'll mention at least a tidbit. The evacuation hospital was the first to enter Manila and give aid to our wounded. During the fierce fighting, which took weeks to free Manila, Dr. Parker and his surgical peers often operated for twenty-four hours straight without sleep. The entire staff was awarded a Presidential Citation for their work. This hospital staff was also the first to enter Japan when the Japanese surrendered. After three months of occupation they returned home.

Within two weeks Dr. Parker started working in a four-man clinic in California. In those days all were required to do some general practice, so he did his share, including many house calls. He delivered our children, and was truly our mentor and best friend.

In 1952 and 1953 he interrupted his work at the clinic and returned to St. Louis University Group of hospitals to complete his training as a specialist in obstetrics and gynecology, after which he returned to California and limited his practice to obstetrics and gynecology. In 1968 he developed hypertension and intolerable headaches. His cardiologist insisted he quit his practice and get into something less demanding. He did, and joined the medical staff of Rockwell's Space Division. After four years, Dr. Parker was promoted to medical director of the division, overseeing the work of the staff physicians and nurses, and was appointed as the private physician for the American and Russian astronauts while they trained at Rockwell.

In 1975 he suffered a severe heart attack while playing tennis in a tournament. His heart was so damaged that in a few days it developed an unusually large aneurysm of the left ventricle. He was in the intensive care unit of a university hospital for two months, attached to a crude heart pump that is no longer used. As a last resort a cardiac surgeon told Dr. Parker's wife, Mable, that Dr. Parker was going to die unless the aneurysm could be surgically removed; he cautioned Mable that Dr. Parker might not survive the procedure.

Dr. Parker survived the surgery but had a stormy recovery. Because of recurrent heart failure, he spent two years in a hospital bed at home. Slowly regaining strength, he began working at free prenatal clinics for a few hours one or two days a week, until he was able to do more. He began teaching nurses and doctors to perform proper prenatal examinations, and later became the prenatal consultant for the city of Long Beach, California. There he was instrumental in setting up an expanded training program for registered nurses who wanted to become nurse practitioners in the field of obstetrics.

Dr. Parker retired in June 2000. Today he still plays tennis twice a week—doubles only, and no running for balls or jumping to hit one.

William Bockus, B.B.A., B.S., M.E.D., Ph.D.

Preface

The purpose of this book is to encourage readers to function creatively and to open their eyes to opportunity, so that they can truly get more out of their lives by learning from the problems of patients of mine.

The book is written in three sections. The first section contains a variety of case histories on diverse subjects. All are true and derive from my private practice; the names have been changed in some cases, but nothing else. My thoughts are interspersed.

The second is about patients who are suffering terribly, not from illness, but from the inability to handle life's everyday difficulties. They can mold their lives for better or worse, depending on how they respond to stress. Excerpts from medical articles and books on medicine are included, as are case histories of many people whom I have treated. Among these are mental and physical disabilities, as well as drug-related complications.

The third section, "Keys to Slavery," is an explicit treatise on dangerous drugs. Their use and their terrible consequences are given in case histories reported in the medical literature and from the clinics I worked in. Included are heartbreaking examples of the frantic search for a cure when hope is almost gone.

Section One

Chapter 1

My First Circumcision

As seniors in medical school in 1939, we were taught to circumcise male infants after the tenth day following birth—some bright doctor had made a study showing that infants' blood clotted faster after the tenth day of life. Also, we were told to schedule the operation on either a Saturday or Sunday so as not to interfere with our attending classes.

It was snowing on this particular Saturday morning, and I had to take a long streetcar ride from my boarding house near the medical school to Hooverville on the edge of the Mississippi River. This shantytown was named for President Hoover, whom most blamed for the depression we were in. I was dressed in my best and only suit, clean white shirt, tie, and shabby coat. The Homburg on my head was only good for "window dressing." I still remember how uncomfortable I felt, stared at by the poor people on the streetcar—especially the young girls, who giggled and furtively pointed to my shiny black bag, which I held firmly in my hands. No one said anything.

At the ride's end I still had five blocks to walk. The blizzard was at its height. When I arrived at the dilapidated shack of cardboard and scraps of lumber, I was stiff from cold. I knocked on the flimsy door, and was answered by a very loud, "Come in." I entered and was greeted by a gruff, "Who are you?"

"I'm the doctor; I've come to circumcise your son."

A huge hulk of a man sat by a hot potbelly stove next to the kitchen table, a can of beer in his hand, his red eyes staring at me for the longest time. Finally, he said, "Shit—you're no doctor, you're not old enough to change a diaper."

"Yes, I am a doctor, I delivered your son in there," pointing to the tiny bedroom where eleven days ago I had attended his wife. "Where's your wife? She'll tell you."

"Shit, I don't know where she went. I almost kicked her ass this morning for drinking most of my beer. She took the kids with her to get some food and more beer. She'll be back before she freezes her ass out there in the cold."

"May I wash my hands before I start?" I asked.

"Help yourself," he replied, pointing to the kitchen sink, which was full of dirty dishes. I put aside enough of them to make room for my hands. While scrubbing I silently hoped that all would go well. I had observed four circumcisions, but this would be my first to do—and I was all alone.

"Do you have some clean towels?" I asked.

"What for?"

"I'll need them so I don't spill blood on the table."

"Blood! You bastard, you better not spill any of my son's blood, I'll kill you if you do."

I was hoping he couldn't see the beads of cold sweat that I felt forming on my forehead. With faked authority I responded, "Don't worry, everything's going to be fine. Now spread the big towel on the kitchen table, we'll put your son on it. I want you to sit down at the head of the table and hold him so he won't move."

He finished his beer, burped loudly, and sat down. I showed him how to hold his son's legs apart so that I had room to work. I washed and prepared the penile area. With trepidation and a silent prayer I sat opposite him to circumcise the child. I applied the first clamp to the foreskin and, predictably, the infant let out a painful cry. The father looked up at me and, with a mean eye, said, "You know what you're doing?"

"Oh, yes," I said, applying the second clamp a few millimeters to the side of the first. Holding the two clamps in my left hand, I picked up a metal probe with my right and separated the foreskin. The child continued to bellow without letup. The father stared at me mercilessly. I took the scissors and cut the foreskin between the clamps. A drop or two of blood fell on the father's fingers. Instantly, he turned pale, let go of the child, and his head hit the table with a thump that opened a three-inch gash in his forehead.

Just then his wife walked in with a sack of beer and groceries, four children behind her. I sure was glad to see her. She helped me put her staggering husband on the bed while one of the children held the infant on the table. I pulled some sterile gauze pads out of my black bag, and applied them to the husband's laceration, then instructed one of the children to apply pressure to the gauze on her father's wound until I could finish circumcising the baby. With the mother holding the infant I completed the circumcision quickly and without problem.

By now the father had roused completely and was most cooperative. After cleansing his wound and numbing it with Novocain, I put five stitches in his forehead to close the laceration.

"You're the greatest, Doc," he said twice. "Now, we got to have a beer together to celebrate my son's circumcision."

I drank a sip or two and thanked him, gave the couple instruction on care of the circumcision, plus a date for them to come to our clinic for removal of the father's stitches. Then I said, "Goodbye and good luck" and left.

Heading home on the streetcar, I felt great. If this was what being a doctor meant, I couldn't have chosen a greater profession. I sat tall in my seat and thanked God that I hadn't fumbled.

Chapter 2
Internship

In June 1940, at age twenty-two—two weeks after graduating from medical school and just ten days after wedding Mable—I began fifty-two weeks of confinement that I'll never forget. I was shut up in a 350-bed teaching hospital in Ohio, along with eleven other interns and twelve resident physicians. We were only allowed to leave the hospital every other weekend. One had to complete a year of internship to receive a medical license allowing one to open an office and practice medicine.

If you decided to become a specialist, for example in surgery, internal medicine, urology, or pediatrics, you had to compete to be admitted to the hospital of your choice anywhere in the United States. Those with the highest grades had the best chance of getting into the better hospitals. Every month during internship, you were graded and received a report card with comments on your work from the "staff"—the doctors who were our teachers and oversaw all our work. They were all specialists, had private offices in town, and sent their own patients to this hospital. Approximately one-third of the patients in this hospital were classed as "poor" and were never billed by the hospital, or the staff doctors, or by us poor interns and residents. We interns were paid by the hospital: $20.00 per month plus free room and laundry. The residents received a few dollars more.

I was all set to see my first patient as an intern. Sporting white shirt, pants, shoes, and coat, from which a stethoscope peeked out of the left pocket, I stepped into room 224. "Good morning, Mr. Crane, I'm Doctor Parker. I've come to take your history and examine you."

"Oh, Jesus," he responded with a barely audible, deep, painful sigh. "Get me a doctor, I don't want to die."

"I am a doctor, and I'll do my best to get you well."

Moving his head ever so slightly, he grumbled, "You're not old enough to be a doctor." Tears were rolling down his cheeks. "Get me a real doctor who can take this poison out of me. Please, please, PLEASE."

"I'll get a specialist to see you, but first I must get a good history, draw some blood, and have you give me a urine specimen. Then I've got to take it to the laboratory and check it all out. The specialist won't see you until all this is done. O.K.?"

"Aw-right," he mumbled.

"What childhood diseases did you have?" I asked.

"Oh, shit, what's the difference? Just take out the poison. I don't want to die!"

"Poison, what do you mean?" I anxiously asked.

"I tried to kill myself, so I drank the poison."

"What was the name of the poison?" I asked.

"Kal-ka-haln-kal-kaalme" he stuttered.

"Rest a minute, I can't understand you. I'll give you a shot first to stop your pain." I called the nurse and told her to give him a quarter grain of morphine. In the meantime, I checked his blood pressure and pulse and listened to his heart. All were normal except for some fresh blood staining his teeth.

The nurse arrived and injected the morphine. I asked her to bring in the laboratory tray, which contained syringes, needles, test tubes, and a Foley catheter for obtaining a urine specimen. In those days the intern had to draw the blood, catheterize the patient with the Foley if he couldn't void, then take the specimens to the laboratory and examine all of them under the pathologist's scrutiny. All intravenous medication had to be started by the intern.

After completing the lab work, I returned to the patient. His response was now much weaker and I was unable to understand his utterances. I left the room and called the second-year resident for help. He arrived promptly. I described my patient's signs and symptoms and emphasized that he had tried to commit suicide by swallowing a poison. He couldn't get out its name, and kept saying something like "Kal-ka-kahn-kalme" over and over.

The resident interrupted me and said, "He was trying to tell you he swallowed Calomel, which is mercuric chloride. It's poisonous in a most corrosive way. I'll examine him right away; meantime, run up to the lab and ask the pathologist to check for mercuric chloride in the blood and urine you took up earlier. I'll stay here with the patient until you get back."

Returning to the room some ten minutes later with the ominous report from the pathologist, I immediately told the resident, "Both the blood and urine contain mercury."

The resident put his hand on my shoulder and pointed to the door. The patient never moved. I don't know if he heard me say, "Mercury in the blood and urine." In the hallway, out of hearing range of the patient, the resident said to me, "Ed, never again blurt out a lab finding where a patient can hear. You must first discuss the findings with a resident physician. Then we can tell the patient, in a caring way, at the opportune time." He continued, "I'm sorry, Ed, the prognosis for your patient is hopeless, but he's still your patient and you must continue to treat him. He'll die in a few days from corrosive lesions. He's going to bleed from every organ in his body. You must help him be as comfortable as you can make him. Never hesitate to call me if you're not sure what to do."

"Should I wash out his stomach to retrieve some of the poison?" I asked the resident.

"It's too late, Ed. He took the poison twenty-four hours ago. The mercuric chloride has all been absorbed, and it's in all the organs of the body. When I examined him, he'd already started bleeding from ulcers in his mouth and throat. His kidneys will shut down in a day or two and then there'll be no urine, just blood. All you can do, Ed, is feed him intravenously, and give him oxygen continually to help him breathe easier. Don't hesitate to inject morphine whenever he wants it. Talk to his family and tell them the whole truth. Sorry, Ed. Call me anytime."

I was profoundly shocked, and can still remember the patient's agonizing plea for help. He died seventy-two hours later; I was holding his hand at the time.

With the help of the police, about two weeks after his death, I found out what had happened. Some unknown person had called the police and told them that a man was lying on a bench in a nearby park. The police arrived and my patient told them he'd drunk poison the previous night. Now it was near noon. He was unable to say much more. The pain was crippling. The police found no identification in his pockets, so they brought him directly to our hospital. Later, the police were able to determine that he was twenty years of age and had left home in Iowa two years earlier. He now lived with an abandoned alcoholic man in a rickety shack on the edge of the Mississippi River. He'd never married, and had no brothers or sisters. He couldn't find work, so he tried to kill himself. His parents were notified, but they never responded.

Chapter 3

Residency

After exposure to all specialties during my internship, I concluded that obstetrics and gynecology (OB-GYN) was the only kind of work I wanted to do for the rest of my life. It was the work I enjoyed most. Obstetrics, in almost all cases, ended happily: the new mother beamed, the father would hand out cigars to all the men around, pat the doctor on the back, and thank him over and over. Yes, there were tragedies, and not all labors had happy endings. These hurt me very much; though they were inevitable, they nonetheless caused pain for the family and me.

Gynecology gave me the opportunity to do major surgery. For some reason, I felt at ease while operating. I believed early that I had an inborn "knack" for surgery, but I soon found out that my assumption was wrong. Excellence takes work—endless years of it.

At about the same time, Ignace Paderewski, a Polish pianist who had won fame and fortune as one of the greatest concert performers of all time, gave a concert in New York City. After its conclusion, an American pianist approached Paderewski and said, "I would give my life to play the piano like you do."

"I did," Paderewski answered, and walked away. He died the following year, 1941, at seventy-eight. This incident made an unforgettable impression on me.

I delivered many babies, and performed three or more surgeries every day for 360 days. We residents did get off work three nights a week. On these nights of freedom we were permitted to make "house calls" for the hospital's staff physicians. Doing this supplemented our meager salary. We could keep the five dollars we made for each house call. Hell, for five bucks I could take my wife to dinner at a good restaurant and have ten cents left to buy a pack of cigarettes!

At the conclusion of one year of residency, I volunteered for the army. Not until the end of WWII was I able to conclude the other two years of my OB-GYN specialty. I made my share of house calls, and even treated private patients of one of our staff physicians at his office when he didn't want to work some nights.

At five p.m. one day I was getting ready to go home, as it was my night off. A staff physician asked if I could make a house call for him before I went home. "All you have to do," he said, "is give him a shot. We can go down together to my car and I'll give you a syrette with one-tenth grain of apomorphine in it. Shoot it in his arm and get out of his way or he'll vomit in your face."

A syrette is a collapsible tube with an attached hypodermic needle, for subcutaneous injection of medication. Apomorphine is made from morphine, and when given by injection produces almost instantaneous and powerful projectile vomiting, followed by profound calmness.

"How can I give him a shot? He may not want it," I said.

"Oh, he will. Just tell him I sent you and he must have it. He never wears a shirt at home. You can shoot it in his arm before he has chance to argue. I've done it many times, it always works."

"You're sure he won't hurt me?" I asked.

"He won't hurt you. He just likes to raise hell by shouting at his wife when he's drunk—that's when his wife calls me for help. He's never hit her and she's not afraid of him. Most of the time he really wants the shot—he feels so sorry for his wife."

"O.K., I'll go," I answered, then hesitated and asked, "Why doesn't she call the police?"

"She has, but they won't come unless he hits her," the staff doctor answered.

"O.K.," I said for the second time, and went with him to his car to get the medication.

I made the house call. Everything went as the staff doctor said it would. This was the first and last time I saw so powerful an emetic action, and the calmness that followed frightened me. I thought he might die, but he didn't.

We residents called this type of house call a "doozy!" There were others that were shockers. One went like this: I arrived at a house in a shabby neighborhood and rang the doorbell. A man opened the door, "Who are you?" he asked.

"I'm Doctor Parker."

"I didn't call you," he smarted.

"Yes, I know, but Doctor Smith couldn't come and asked me to make this house call for him."

"Bullshit! You mean he was too lazy to come himself," he blasted.

"Well, if you feel this way, I can go, and you can call whomever you wish," I responded.

"Hell! You're here now, so come in—go upstairs, you'll find her there."

"Who is she, and what's the matter with her?" I asked.

"It's my wife—just go upstairs and into the first bedroom."

Reluctantly, I went up the stairs and stepped into an open bedroom. No one was there. I went into the other bedroom—and no one was there. So, I walked out into the hall to the head of the stairs and shouted, "I can't find her anywhere. Where is she?"

"I told you, she's in the first bedroom, just open the closet door."

I did. There she was, hanging by a rope around her neck, her feet dangling above the floor. A chair lay on its side beside her. Rigor mortis—stiffening of the body after death—had already set in.

I shouted down again, "Hey! Come on up, we have to talk."

He came upstairs, but never said a word, nor even glanced at his dead wife.

"You should have called the police and the undertaker, not a doctor," I said.

"I figured Doctor Smith would do that for me. Can't you?" he asked.

"Yes, I can and will," and I did.

I waited until the police arrived. After telling them what I knew of the event, they dismissed me and I left. I never heard from the police or the husband. Dr. Smith gave me five dollars for making his house call.

On another occasion, a very busy staff doctor named Sawyer asked me to help him treat patients in his office. It was to be for three hours only, from six to nine P.M., once a week, and the pay would be five dollars per hour. It sounded good so I agreed to do it. Together we usually saw ten to fifteen patients in the three hours. Most had the usual colds, sore throats, aching backs, headaches, minor cuts, and bruises. All went smoothly, except that I noticed some patients came in with an empty bottle, gave it to the nurse for a refill, and paid her a dollar. They never saw the doctor. Some nights she was busier than we were. One evening I asked her, "Jane, what is that liquid you sell for a dollar a bottle?"

'"Don't you know?" she responded.

"No, I don't."

"It's medicine Doctor Sawyer makes. Come into the drug room and I'll show you."

She led me into a small room. Three walls were lined with cabinets, and on the other was a sink with a counter on each side. Four of the cabinets were filled with six- and eight-ounce empty bottles. The other cabinets contained stationery, labels, drug samples, utensils, gloves, towels, toilet necessities, and books, etc. On the counter were three pitchers and a funnel; on the floor were three five-gallon bottles. One contained a bright red liquid, one a green liquid, and the third a yellow liquid.

"What's that?" I asked, pointing to the bottles.

"It's Doctor Sawyer's medicine. The red is for nerves, the green is for stomach pain, and the yellow for sleep."

"What's in them?" I asked.

"I don't know. You'd better ask Doctor Sawyer."

At an opportune time, I cornered Dr. Sawyer and asked, "What's in the big bottles, Doctor?"

"It's just clean water, Ed: the red contains a red dye, and I flavor it with peppermint. The green has a green dye and is mint flavored, the yellow has a yellow dye and a vanilla flavor."

"You're kidding me."

"No, I'm not Ed!"

"Do the patients know what they're buying?" I asked.

"Of course not. It's a placebo."

"What's a placebo?" I asked.

"It's an innocuous agent that helps them and can't hurt them. In this case it's only clean water with a bit of coloring."

"Doctor, it's hard for me to believe what you just said."

"It shouldn't be. Hippocrates, the father of medicine, told us 400 years before the birth of Christ that medicine is 50 percent science and 50 percent art."

"Yes, I know," I responded.

"Ed, do you remember the traveling medicine shows when

you were a kid?"

"Yes, I do, and I remember them proclaiming that they could cure everything from insomnia to impotence."

"That's right, Ed, they knew how to cure. They played happy music, they danced, and they sang out loud to counteract depression brought on by illness. They generated hope by anecdotal testimonials, and tried their best to convince you that their medicine was a natural substance extracted from plants. The entire show made it easy to sell a worthless remedy, but most importantly, it also ensured the placebo effect. We don't understand how the placebo effect works, but we know for certain that it brings about improvement in one-third of the patients. It's been proven by double-blind studies. My medicine works the same way. It's a placebo," he finished.

"You've convinced me, Doc," I muttered.

Postscript

I administered apomorphine only once in my entire career, because treating that patient with it in 1942 frightened me so much. I recently attended a symposium in San Diego, California. One of the many subjects discussed in this updated review of medical practice was erectile dysfunction (ED), the inability to achieve and maintain an erection for completion of sexual intercourse. Today, ED is often treated successfully with tablets of sildenafil citrate (brand name Viagra). Through a combination of enzymatic reactions, smooth muscle in the penis is relaxed, which makes blood rush in, causing an erection. It doesn't work for everyone, but you can discuss several other options with your physician. Today, Viagra is the only FDA-approved drug for treating ED. In Europe, however, apomorphine is available to treat it, administered in two-milligram doses—much smaller than what's used in the United States as a powerful emetic.

Don't you think that the patient I injected with apomorphine knew by then that he'd become totally relaxed and soon respond with an erection that he and his wife both looked forward to? Apomorphine usually takes twenty to thirty minutes to produce this effect—but so does Viagra. It took the medical profession more than fifty years to recognize this salutary effect of apomorphine, and in June 2000 the FDA denied it approval for treating ED. The request for its approval was resubmitted four months later, but there has been no response as yet.

How slowly we learn!

Chapter 4

Launching a Practice

"Who told you I needed an assistant?" he asked, and then added, "Please sit down."

Coughing lightly to clear my throat, I answered, "Sister Liguori at St. Luke's Hospital."

"Hmm, I guess being supervisor of the hospital isn't enough work for her; now she's running an employment agency."

"Perhaps I should explain, Doctor Haines," I said.

"Just call me Serge, everyone does," he said softly.

"Yes, sir," I replied, and continued, "I made a point to see Sister Liguori yesterday. My wife and I had already decided that this was the town we wanted to live in. All I needed was to find a place to work. The local hospital seemed the logical place to inquire, and that's how and where I met Sister Liguori. She was most courteous, and even though I know I was crowding her busy schedule, she let on as if I were the only person who mattered. She certainly has a charming personality."

"Oh, she's a charmer all right," said Serge, with an inscrutable smile.

He muttered something else, but I couldn't make it out and felt it was best not to ask, so I continued. "Well, I asked her which doctors she thought might be looking for help, and whom she would suggest I contact. She gave me the names of several doctors in the area, but somehow she always came back to you."

"She did, did she?" he spurted.

Despite his utterance, I was sure I detected an expression of sheer delight on his face. "She said you were by far the busiest of them all, and added that if she needed surgery, you'd be the only one she would want operating on her."

"Don't believe all she says; remember she's a charmer."

"She did warn me about you, too."

"Oh? How's that?"

"She said you were a stubborn Dutchman, and might be hard to work with."

"She said that! I'll bet she forgot to tell you she was a spy for the pope."

"She didn't mention it," I answered with a smile.

"Where did you get your training, Doctor Parker?"

"Ed, please."

"All right, where did you go to school, Ed?"

"St. Louis University." I was beginning to feel a bit uncomfortable. Maybe I'd made a mistake coming here. After all, Dr. Haines looked old enough to be my father. If he'd been as busy as Sister Liguori said, he probably hadn't kept up with the progress of medicine.

"Saint Louie!" he half shouted. "That's a top medical center. I've been there several times. Let's see, you had Doctor Doisy, he won the Nobel Prize in physiology and medicine in 1943, just two years ago. His isolation of the estrogenic substance opened up a whole new field of medicine. I'm sure few people realize the importance of his outstanding contribution. You know, Ed, I have this feeling that there are still hundreds of hormones to be discovered, and it will be in this field that the cause of cancer and even the answer to the aging process will be found."

"I hope so, Serge, we're certainly ignorant of the causes today."

"I envy you young doctors. For the first time in history you have some real tools to work with in medicine. You have no idea how much sweat and tears we older men shed before we had sulfa drugs and penicillin. Hell, we treated pneumonia and most infectious diseases with a silent prayer and generous amounts of sympathy. The crap we dispensed was mostly useless colored water and foul-tasting powders and pills. But, in spite of our futile and worthless ministrations, Mother Nature healed most of the sick we attended."

"You're much too modest, Serge."

"I don't think so." He walked behind me and brought out a text. "Recognize this, Ed?"

"Yes, it's Doctor Kuntz's *Textbook of Neuroanatomy.* He was one of my instructors in school. Do you know him?"

"Not really, but I know his book and refer to it whenever I'm handling a tough neurological case. He replaced the book in the bookcase behind his desk and handed me a much larger text. "This is my favorite," he said. "Rose and Carliss' *Surgery,* edited by William Coughlin, M.D."

"Yes, Coughlin was my instructor too; you know he died in 1939."

"Yes, I do. Now there was a surgeon who knew how to handle any type of case. Hell, I saw him remove a brain tumor, a glioblastoma as large as an orange, in less than an hour! Then he walked right into the next operating room and took out a gall bladder in just fifteen minutes. I actually saw him do five major cases that morning. You know, he no sooner finished with the last operation than he strutted right out and made rounds with the interns and residents for two hours before he sat down to rest. I was exhausted just watching him."

"You said it, Serge. Exhaustion was what we all complained of, working with him. When he had his coronary, it took the combined efforts of all the nuns and the medical staff to keep him in bed. He kept insisting he could at least make rounds. He lived about two weeks after his heart attack and was alert to the very end. I was on duty early in the evening about three days before he died. His attending physician had just finished examining him and had gone back to the nurses' station, where he told the nun in charge that Dr. Coughlin was dying. In a few minutes, at least a dozen nuns walked into his room en masse with lighted candles and began praying out loud. Coughlin rose up from bed and shouted, "Quiet! I'm trying to sleep." I never saw a faster exodus.

"That sounds like him all right. Tell me, Ed, did he really have as bad a temper as I've heard he had?"

"Oh, he had a temper, that no one can deny, but you soon learned to disregard it. He was such an exceptional teacher and master surgeon that you could forget his occasional nasty outbursts."

"You know, Ed, I once heard that he threw a tray of surgical instruments out of a sixth-floor window when he got mad at a nurse who kept handing him the wrong instruments while he was operating. Is that true?"

"I don't know, Serge, I've heard the same story...it could be true."

The door opened and a young nurse popped in. "Doctor Haines, Sister Liguori is calling to remind you that you have a ten o'clock surgery. It's five minutes to ten now."

"Tell her to say ten Hail Marys; I'll be there before she finishes."

He rose unhurriedly and stretched his arms. "What did you say your specialty was, Ed?"

"I didn't, but it's obstetrics and gynecology."

He glanced at me resolutely while pausing to put on his coat. His voice was courteous. "There isn't enough OB-GYN here to keep you busy. You'd have to do your share of general practice. However, I don't think it's going to be long before you could limit yourself to your specialty. This town is growing rapidly, and most newcomers are young couples—they breed like rabbits."

"I know, Serge, and I don't mind doing my share of G.P.—after all, that's what I did in the army the past three years."

"Fine. I'd better run along before Sister calls again. Leave your curriculum vitae with Dorothy—she's the secretary. I'll tell her to have one of my nurses show you around the office and I'll get in touch with you in a few days." He shook my hand and added, "It was nice meeting you, Ed. I hope we can work together. Don't worry, I'll call you."

"Thanks, and good luck with your surgery."

Driving to the motel where my wife, Mable, and my daughter, Judy, were waiting, I couldn't help feeling good. The interview went well, I thought, and barring some unforeseen development, the position was mine. It would be so good to settle down and start a practice, after such a long fight to get here. Let's see, after high school there was college, then four years of medical school, followed by internship and residency, and then three years in the U.S. Army Medical Corps—two of them spent in the steaming jungles of New Guinea. It sure took a lot of years to get here. Yes, sir, and it was worth it! I've got the training, the ability, and the confidence; I can't miss. I then realized I was speaking aloud and there was no one in the car with me. Luckily I was in sight of the motel, or I might have been cited for driving under the influence.

"Hi, Daddy! Can we go to the zoo now?"

"Hi, Judy, hello, Mable. Let's go, darlings."

"Daddy, could we see the monkeys first?"

"Anything you want, sweetheart."

It was an exciting day, charged by the endless enthusiasm and energy of a five-year-old. Darkness had fallen before Judy fell asleep in the car on the way back to the motel. Only then were Mable and I able to talk.

"Do you think you'll like working with Serge?" she asked.

"I believe so. He's well trained and fully aware of what's going on in medicine. He has a very warm personality underneath a tough exterior. I found him easy to talk with."

"How old do you think he is?" asked Mable.

"It's hard to tell. He looks young, but I know that he was in World War I, and he mentioned that he has a son who's a freshman in med school at Stanford University. He must be in his fifties, but you'd never know it."

"That's not old."

"I agree, and in fact I'm looking forward to learning from his years of experience. By the way, I also met his assistant, Dr. Art Toy. He's a Dutchman too, very jolly and obviously happy to be working with Serge. He was with him for two years before the war, and then rejoined him just before Japan surrendered. I would have liked to talk longer with Art, but he had an emergency call to make, so we had to cut it short. He should be fun to work with; I'm sure you'll like him."

"What's the office like?"

"It's beautiful! A nurse by the name of Ruth—I can't recall her last name—showed it to me. It's a two-story white stucco building on a corner. Directly across the street is a huge orange grove that backs up against the mountains. The highest peak is Mount Wilson, where the world-famous observatory is located. You can actually see the tower from the office."

"I can't wait to see it."

"You'll love it; it's like a postcard of Switzerland. But let me tell you about the clinic. The rooms are all large, and except for the surgery and X-ray suites, they all have large picture windows facing the mountains. The building is designed so the basement and the second floor can easily be converted into more doctors' offices. At present the second floor has a small, unoccupied apartment, and the basement is empty. The equipment is of the latest design and best quality. The drug and supply rooms are fully stocked with the newest drugs and instruments. I was really impressed with the setup."

"It sounds marvelous. Did Serge give you any idea of when he would call?"

"He said in a few days. I guess he'll be checking my credentials.

I left my curriculum vitae with Dorothy, his secretary."

"I hope it doesn't take long. Judy is good, but I hate to keep her in this small motel room for long. She needs to get out and play with children her age."

"I hope so too, Mable. In the meantime, let's try to have some fun. How about going to the beach tomorrow? I'd like to try my luck at some fishing."

The days passed swiftly, but my mind never stopped working. I tried not to let my worries show, but each evening when we got back from a day's outing, I checked with the motel clerk and got the same answer: "No calls." It was becoming more and more difficult to remain optimistic. In the meantime, I had interviews with four other doctors in the surrounding areas, but in each case there was something lacking. Like Sister Liguori, who would have only Serge if she needed surgery, I found myself refusing all offers. I kept telling myself that Serge would call.

On the eleventh day, there was a message: "Call Serge." My practice was launched.

Chapter 5

My First House Call: Scarlet Fever vs. Constipation

I had been in private practice only a few days when Serge asked me to make a house call for him. A patient had called him earlier that morning and was very concerned about his daughter. Serge had promised the caller that he would stop by in the next hour to see the child. In the meantime, the hospital called Serge about a surgical emergency, so he asked me to make the call for him.

I picked up my shiny new black bag, got into my second-hand

Dodge, and hoped it would make it up the mountain. The salesman from whom I'd bought the car had assured me that it was safe, sound, and reliable, even though the odometer registered over 90,000 miles.

It was a gorgeous morning. The air was clear, and had a fresh scent of orange blossoms. I could see for miles, and the sky was a solid blue overhead. I was relaxed and enjoying the view, especially the flowering Yucca trees, which from a distance looked like a group of hikers making their way up the mountain.

The house, a modest redwood structure surrounded by Eucalyptus trees, was located at the top of a graded and partly paved road that twisted for three miles above our office. It stood alone on about a half acre of flat space carved out of the steep mountains. A small dog barked and snapped as I walked gingerly on a dirt path to the front door. I was greeted with a harsh, "Where's Serge—my husband called *him*."

"Serge couldn't come, he had to rush to an emergency call at the hospital, and asked me to see your child. I'm Serge's new associate; my name is Doctor Parker."

"Come in, she's in the back." I was led without comment through the living room, down a long hall and into the bedroom.

"Jenny, this is Doctor Parker. He came to see you and will try to help you."

"Where is Serge? I want *him* to look at me," she said.

"Serge will see you later, Jenny, if needed. He wanted to come, but he had to rush to the hospital to help someone who couldn't wait," I answered.

"I don't care. I want Serge, not you," she cried. Obviously I wasn't making a good impression with either one; something had to be done.

"Look," I said, taking a shiny silver dollar out of my pocket. I flipped it in the air, caught it, and put my clenched fists together. "Guess which hand it's in." Slowly, Jenny sat up, wiped the tears from her face, and pointed to my right hand. I opened it—no silver dollar. I opened the other hand—no silver dollar.

"Where did it go?" she asked.

"Here it is, on your pillow," I pointed. She picked it up and returned it to me with a quizzical smile. "Now, we'll look at you and see if can make your sickness disappear, O.K.?"

"O.K., but don't hurt me."

"I won't."

I placed my hand on her forehead. Her skin was hot and dry. "Does your head hurt, Jenny?"

"Yeah. Mommy gave me an aspirin, but it still hurts."

"Does anything else hurt you?"

"My throat hurts, especially when I swallow." I turned to her mother and asked, "Did she eat anything today?"

"All she would eat was a little oatmeal and orange juice, but threw it up a few minutes later. She seemed fine last night, but wouldn't eat her dinner."

"Jenny, open your mouth, please." Jenny responded without hesitation. Her throat was flushed. "Stick your tongue out, honey." It had the appearance of a large red strawberry, so characteristic of the disease. In her neck I felt swollen, tender glands on each side, but when I checked her ears they appeared normal.

"Jenny, I'd like to take your temperature, and while we're doing that I'll listen to your heart and feel your tummy, O.K.?" She accepted the thermometer without question. On exposing her trunk, the characteristic rash was visible. Her skin was covered with a fine granular eruption. When I drew my fingertips over the surface of the skin it felt very much like gooseflesh. Each bump was no larger than a pinhead. The eruption spread slightly to the neck and outward upon the extremities. Jenny's face was flushed, but free of the rash. I took out my stethoscope and listened to her heart: it was racing at about 120 beats per minute, but the rhythm was regular. Her lungs were clear. Her abdomen was soft, and even though I pressed over each organ I noted no expression of pain on her face. After checking her reflexes and finding them normal, I took the thermometer from under her tongue and noted that it registered 105° F.

"Jenny, you have scarlet fever, but it's nothing to worry about. I'll write you a prescription that will make you feel better. I want you to drink a lot—that'll make you feel cooler—and will you promise to stay in bed?"

"Do I have to stay in bed?"

"Yes, its very important that you do." I was putting away my thermometer and stethoscope when Jenny spoke out. "I'm seven years old, Can you show me that trick again?" I showed her the trick three more times.

"I have to go now, Jenny, but Serge or I will see you tomorrow."

"O.K., but can you come?"

"O.K.," I answered. I walked into the living room with her mother and sat down to write a prescription for the newest sulfa drug.

"Jenny is to take two of these pills every six hours for one week, and you, your husband, and your other children should also take them." I stopped to ask, "By the way, how many other children do you have, and how old are they."

"Twin girls ten years old, and a boy, twelve."

"Fine. Each of you will take two pills a day for ten days. This should protect you from getting the disease. All the instructions will be on the bottle."

"I'll see that they take them. Say, why does Jenny's face look so funny, Doctor?"

"What do you mean?" I asked.

"Well, didn't you notice? Her face is so red, and yet around her mouth it's so white, she looks like a clown. And another thing: I know she's sick, but I've never seen her eyes look so bright and happy."

"Yes, I did notice. The red face is due to the high fever. The whiteness around the mouth is called 'circumoral pallor.' It's characteristic of scarlet fever, but I don't know why that area is white when the rest of the face is so red. The brightness of the eyes is caused by the stimulating effect of the toxin that's in her system now, being produced by the hemolytic *streptococcus* bacteria that causes scarlet fever." I'm not sure she understood my explanation, but she didn't question me. I went on to describe how the disease was transmitted by droplet infection, and contracted by kissing, or being sprayed by a cough or sneeze. I added that since these same infected droplets of saliva were deposited on the eating utensils and dishes Jenny used, they would have to be washed separately and used only by her.

"How long do we have to be careful?" she asked.

"Until the rash is gone," I answered.

"And how long is that?"

"Usually three to four days."

"She can play then?"

"Well, yes, providing there are no complications."

"Complications! What complications?"

"Sometimes, but not very often, they can get ear infections or even kidney trouble, but don't worry—we'll watch her closely. She's a healthy girl."

"You sure she's going to be alright?"

"I'll do my best. Now I'd like you to give her an aspirin and repeat it every four hours, until her temperature is below 100° F. Also, give her a sponge bath with lukewarm water. It will cool her off. Please call me at any time if you're worried." She thanked me and walked me to the front door. Leaving, I said, "Jenny will be all right. See you tomorrow."

Later that day I told Serge about Jenny's illness. The following morning, the first call our receptionist got was one instructing Serge and me, in no uncertain terms, not to bother making another call at the house. She did add that Jenny was well. At the end of the month the usual five-dollar statement for a house call was sent out. In a few days Serge received a letter:

Dear Serge,

You have been my doctor for 15 years. We have always called you, and no one else, when anybody was sick. Last month I called you when Jenny was sick. You promised to come, but instead, without asking me, you sent some young fellow who claimed to be your assistant. He scared the hell out of my wife and had her scrubbing everything and wouldn't allow Jenny to play with her brother and sisters. He even told her to use separate dishes. Well, Jenny was no better the next day. She still had a temperature of 104°. So I called Dr. Wiltse and asked him to see her. He came himself, no substitutes, and looked at my child and felt her belly and right away knew what was wrong. He said she was constipated and that's why her skin was so broken out and her fever so high. He gave her an enema himself and told my wife to repeat it in the evening. Well, by morning Jenny's rash was gone, her fever was gone and she wanted to eat and play. Now I'm writing to you to tell you that I'm not going to pay you the $5.00 for the house call your associate made. In the first place, I never asked for him, and in the second place I don't think he is a doctor. He couldn't be, otherwise he would know the difference between scarlet fever and constipation. I hope this settles the matter.

Your longtime patient,

Ernie

Serge handed me the letter. I couldn't believe what I was reading. Tears welled up in my eyes, and I had a difficult time hiding them.

"Ed," Serge spoke up, "don't let it get you down. You're going to meet more people like Ernie, and you have to realize that logic and rational behavior is something foreign to them. They're the prime targets of the smooth-talking charlatan, and there's no master of this art like Doctor Wiltse. He speaks with the authority of the ignorant. I'll tell you about him, but for now, why don't you take the rest of the day off?"

"Thanks, Serge, I appreciate that. But if you don't mind, I'd rather go back to work."

Chapter 6
Foreign Bodies

In a current issue of a popular medical journal, an article appeared about a young man who was brought into an emergency room in a stuporous state. Soon after arrival he had a series of grand-mal convulsions, after which he vomited explosively. The friends who'd brought him in insisted on being with him in the treatment room. As a consequence, they not only witnessed some of the most grotesque, life-threatening fits, but also became the inadvertent targets of his projectile vomiting. Startled by the sudden dramatic events, and obviously concerned for his life, they volunteered that he had just returned from Columbia, South America. Without prompting, they added that before leaving the country he had swallowed over 100 condoms containing cocaine.

An X-ray was taken before he was admitted to the intensive care unit. The bags of cocaine were readily visible in the colon. Undoubtedly one or more of the bags had leaked or ruptured, allowing the cocaine to be absorbed and to poison him. He required artificial respiration, intravenous feeding, and various other life-support measures before he was out of danger. In case you're wondering, the cocaine-filled rubbers were recovered by induced vomiting, purges, and enemas.

The young man spent ten days in the hospital and, except for some residual sore sphincters, all he had to worry about now was:

1. *Possible retribution from the cocaine dealers*
2. *A fine*
3. *A jail sentence*
4. *Hospital and doctors bills*

Of course, he would never get any sympathy from Dr. Condom, the eighteenth-century English physician who invented the rubber and for whom the device is named. The good doctor must have labored night after night until he came upon the idea of covering the penis with a sheath of rubber to prevent conception and protect against venereal disease. His discovery liberated men and women from responsibility and suffering, and gave us license to enjoy sex. It was a tremendous medical breakthrough, for which Condom quietly received worldwide acclaim. I'm sure he would turn over in his grave if he knew some fool had swallowed his invention for the purpose of transporting drugs. Now, that's how a condom became a "foreign body." The following case history will illustrate how a simple toy balloon became one, too.

I was sitting at my desk at the office one evening, trying to catch up on some paperwork, but not getting very far. I was tired. It had been a long day: The first call came in at one a.m. Mrs. Carhitus was having pain every five minutes. After quieting her and determining that she was in labor, I said, "Have Dave take you to the hospital, Mary, and I'll meet you there shortly."

Now, I don't mind getting up at five in the morning; by then I've had enough sleep, but one a.m. is bad. I'm in my deepest coma then, and when roused, tend to be short tempered for the remainder of the day.

Mary delivered a healthy baby girl before three a.m. Ordinarily, I'd have gone back to bed, but just then, two other nice ladies decided to have their babies, so I remained at the hospital and delivered them. By the time I was finished, the sun was halfway up in the sky, and I still had a hysterectomy to do before I could go home, change clothes, and get to the office—sleep was out of the question.

The office calls went smoothly; even though I was running late all day, no one complained. There's something about obstetrical patients that sets them apart. They seem to understand that the delay in being seen is unintentional. Perhaps they sense that they themselves would someday foul up the office schedule. Whatever the reason, they're tolerant and wonderful.

The building was empty now, everyone had been seen, and all I had to do was some dictating and charting. I would much rather have gone home, but Serge, my senior partner, had years ago drilled into me the importance of keeping patient records up to date. He had an iron-willed habit of never putting off an important task. He couldn't understand why everyone wasn't like him, and had no patience with procrastinators. So, from force of habit, I stayed on, completing the charts, but secretly I cursed him that night. "Hell, he's almost sixty years old and I'm thirty years younger; why should I keep following his lead, and how the devil does he keep up the pace?" Serge had been the last to leave that day, and as he walked out the door, he said, "Good night, Ed, don't bother going to the hospital tonight—I'll make rounds for you."

I was working on the last chart when I realized I hadn't had dinner. I'd begun to dial my wife when a pounding and kicking on the reception door interrupted me. It was just a few steps from where I was sitting. I went to the door and asked, "Who's there?"

"Help, help!" I released the lock, and there stood a young woman holding a child in her arms. "Help me! Help me!" she cried, and suddenly thrust the child into my arms. One look at the child convinced me his condition was critical. He was an ashen color and was laboring to breathe.

"Come! Follow me," I shouted, while hurrying down the hall and into the surgery. Placing the child on the operating table, I worked a small, firm pillow under his shoulders, so I could fully extend his head.

"Hold his arms against his head, like this," I demonstrated. She didn't move from where she was standing at the foot of the table, but instead started screaming hysterically. The noise was deafening.

"God damn it, shut up! Come here and hold his arms like I said, so I can look into his throat, please, and can you tell me what happened?" She was speechless. Trembling and sobbing, she managed to hold his arms and keep his head still. I pulled over a stool to the head of the operating table, sat down, and, from an adjacent surgical tray, picked up the laryngoscope, which is nothing more than a flashlight with an attached metal tongue depressor. Wasting no time, I carefully inserted the instrument into the child's mouth, compressed the tongue, and was able to see the area of the windpipe. Laying over the opening of the trachea was a bright yellow "foreign body." With a sigh of relief and a silent prayer of thanks, I picked up the forceps from the surgical tray and with it lifted a small rubber balloon, which was acting as a cork, off the windpipe. As soon as I removed the balloon, the child's breathing improved and his color returned to a normal pink. Moments later he started to cry, grabbed his mother, and then on cue began to scream.

I got up, put my hand on the mother's shoulder and said, "He'll be fine now." She looked up at me, trying to smile, but her sobbing only got louder, and the boy's screaming never let up for a second. I turned and walked into an adjacent room to rinse my hands and wash the beads of sweat from my forehead. A few minutes later I returned to the surgery. No one was there. I walked into the waiting room. No one was there. I looked into all the rooms, yelling repeatedly, "Where are you?" Then later, "Where the hell did you go?" No answer. Finally, realizing that they'd gone, I turned off the lights, locked up the building, and drove home.

A balloon is just one thing that can become a foreign body when used for a purpose or in a way for which it was not intended. Pins, nails, screws, pieces of glass, fragments of metal, plastic bits, tiny toys, fruit pits, pieces of food, and many other things have all been implicated.

Not long ago, a mother brought her child into our clinic. She was concerned about a cough he'd had for three days. It seems he hacked all day and night, didn't want to eat or drink, and at times almost strangled. When asked why she hadn't brought him in sooner, she replied, "He wasn't running a fever, so I thought it wasn't serious."

An X-ray revealed a needle lodged in his windpipe. Arrangements were made to send him to the hospital immediately. The mother still wasn't convinced that his condition was serious, even though she was shown the X-ray. "It couldn't be serious, he wasn't running a fever," she repeated. That same afternoon, a thoracic surgeon using a bronchoscope removed the needle. The child made an uneventful recovery and went home the following morning.

Perhaps one of the most unusual foreign bodies that I'm aware of was a spoonful of honey. Five siblings were eating breakfast and talking at the same time. One of the youngsters was especially fond of honey and would eat it by the spoonful. He had just filled his mouth with honey when his sister said something that made him gasp. He immediately began choking and struggling to breathe. His mother phoned me and rapidly related the facts, adding, "He's turning blue."

I told her to get him to the floor, turn him on his side, raise his body, but keep his head down. I also instructed her to tell the other children to apply hot, wet towels to his neck and mouth area. I assured her I was on my way, as they lived only a few blocks away. I raced my car to their home. When I arrived, his breathing was already back to normal and his color a healthy pink. Raising the body and lowering the head had allowed the honey to drain away from the windpipe. Applying the hot towels probably helped thin the honey and make it run out more freely.

It can be dangerous to talk or laugh with a mouthful of food, and adults are not immune. I'm sure you are all familiar with the syndrome called "Cafe Coronary." Frequently it happens after the party is well oiled with drink. Conversation is at a hilarious level and appetites are ravenous. The victim usually has a large piece of food in his mouth when he suddenly laughs or tries to speak out. In doing so, he sucks the food into his windpipe. Suddenly he can't speak or breathe, he turns white, then very blue, and collapses. If not relieved, he'll die in five minutes. You are there—what can you do? You can initiate the Heimlich maneuver, named for Dr. Henry J. Heimlich, who first discovered it.

1. *If the victim is standing, get behind him and wrap your arms around his waist. Make a fist with one of your hands and place it an inch or two above the victim's belly button. Put your other hand over your fist, push way in and give a quick upward thrust. Repeat several times if at first unsuccessful.*
2. *If the victim is sitting, you can stand behind his or her chair and do the same maneuver.*
3. *If the victim has already collapsed and is lying on the floor, face the victim and kneel astride his hips. Place the heel of one of your hands on his belly, again just above the belly button, place your other hand on top of the first, and press into the victim's belly with a quick upward thrust. Repeat several times if not at first successful.*

If the Heimlich maneuver should fail, try the following:

Force the victim's mouth open, and put your hand in the mouth. Slide your thumb, middle, and index fingers over the tongue and feel for the blockage, which is usually a large piece of meat. Grasp it with your thumb, middle, and index fingers and bring it out.

Unless you know your anatomy and how to apply it, I can't recommend trying a tracheotomy if all else fails. The Heimlich maneuver usually works, and it does so because there is always air in the lungs. Even after expulsion there is still over a half quart of air left in the lungs. During inspiration, which is when food can become trapped in the windpipe, there are about two quarts of air in the lungs. When you institute the Heimlich maneuver you are literally popping the cork. You can demonstrate this by blowing up a balloon and then inserting a cork in the mouth of the balloon. Suddenly squeeze the balloon and watch the cork pop out.

A word of caution: If you see a victim struggling to breathe, ask her to signal before instituting the Heimlich maneuver. Show her by putting your hand to your own throat and ask her to signal whether she is choking. Remember, it's impossible for a choking victim to talk. A person having a heart attack can sometimes also look like she is choking on food, and she would need cardio-pulmonary resuscitation. The Heimlich maneuver could do harm to the heart attack patient, so make sure before you proceed.

Before closing this chapter on foreign bodies, I'll say a few words about small foreign bodies—especially low-density ones. The ubiquitous aluminum pull-tab is a good example. Next time you're in the park or at the beach, look around; you'll find pull-tabs everywhere on the ground. Unfortunately, toddlers and little children love to pick up these shiny aluminum strips. Invariably, they put them in their mouths, and not infrequently either inhale or swallow them. Most of the time the parent or guardian never sees them in the act.

Last year one California hospital reported treating seven children for complications from swallowing or aspirating pull-tabs. Multiply this by the number of hospitals in the country and you get some idea of the total of these accidents. In the report, one of the seven children bled to death from a hole the pull-tab made in the large artery in his throat. Two others had severe complications that required several operations before they recovered. In all seven cases the parents neither saw nor suspected that their children had swallowed or aspirated the pull-tab. The children were brought to the hospital because they were coughing or had abdominal pain.

Unfortunately, the diagnosis isn't always made promptly. Single X-ray films will frequently not show the pull-tab: like glass and plastic, aluminum pull-tabs are of low density and therefore absorb X-rays poorly. They cast a very faint shadow on X-ray film, which can be missed by the observer. Often, several different views of the same area are required before this type of foreign body can be visualized.

If your child inhales a foreign body, the symptoms will depend on its size. If it's large enough to completely block the opening of the windpipe, it will cause suffocation and death in a few minutes, unless removed. If the object is smaller than the opening of the windpipe, it will work its way down the trachea or even into a lung. The child will develop a cough, the intensity of which will depend on how much irritation and obstruction the foreign body is causing; the cough could be anything from a slight hacking to a choking struggle for life. So, if your child suddenly develops a cough without any previous symptoms of a cold, suspect a foreign body and get him or her to a doctor. Don't attempt to treat your child yourself. Cough syrups are absolutely useless, and pounding on the back may only force the object farther down into the respiratory tree.

What are the symptoms if your child swallows a foreign body? She may have none. If the object is the size of a penny or smaller, and has smooth edges, it will usually pass spontaneously, even in an infant. For confirmation, simply strain each stool until you recover the object. Most foreign bodies will pass within forty-eight hours. An object the size of a nickel or larger may get stuck somewhere along the intestinal tract and have to be removed surgically. If its edges are sharp it can cut the gut and cause bleeding; this too requires surgical intervention. The child will complain of abdominal pain and may pass blood in her stool. She may or may not run a fever.

So, if you have a child who develops these symptoms and you can't account for them, suspect a foreign body and get her to the doctor. Again, don't try home remedies—especially do not give a laxative or enema, which may perforate the bowel and endanger your child's life. Alert your doctor to the fact that your child may have swallowed a foreign body. The doctor can then order more than one view of the suspect area if the original single X-ray film is negative. The physician will appreciate your information, and most importantly, you'll save your child a lot of suffering.

Chapter 7

Infertility

"Good morning, Doctor."

"Good morning, Ruth. Are you feeling any better?"

"I feel fine and ready to work. Your first case is the couple sitting in your consultation room. He insisted you see his wife but wouldn't tell me why. I told him you were booked full this morning, but he insisted they speak to you for just a few minutes, so I told him they could come in at nine a.m. and could stay no longer than fifteen minutes. They were here at eight-thirty. I hope you don't mind—he was so insistent."

"It's O.K., Ruth. I'll talk to them."

Sitting in my consultation room was a couple probably in their late twenties, well dressed and relaxed. After the usual salutations, he got right to the point.

"Doctor, we've been married two years and she can't get pregnant. Several people have told me you were good at treating infertility. I have to leave tomorrow to give a lecture in New York, so I thought you could give Margaret, my wife, an appointment while I'm gone, to see what's wrong with her."

"What are you lecturing about?" I asked.

"Amalgamation of metals; you're very busy this morning, so I won't go into any detail. I'm a chemist by trade. I'll be gone five days, giving some demonstrations at the university."

"That's fine," I answered. "Now, I'd like to ask just a few questions. Are you both well?"

"Yes, we are."

"Any operations?"

"I had my tonsils removed when I was ten. My wife still has hers."

"Any serious illnesses?"

"Never," he answered, and she agreed.

"Whenever I treat infertility, I want first to check the husband to be sure he has motile sperm in adequate numbers. So, if you wish, I'll have my nurse, Ruth, give you a sterile container to take home with you. You can bring it back containing your ejaculate before three p.m. today. I will call you after five p.m. and let you know if you're at fault or not. If you're O.K., your wife can make an appointment to begin her examinations next week. Do you have any questions?"

"No, that makes sense to me. I'll see you get my specimen today. And thanks for seeing us."

The specimen arrived at two p.m. Ruth prepared the slides in our laboratory at once. I confirmed by microscopic examination that the number of sperm was more than adequate, with normal bodies and excellent motility.

I phoned and said, "George, you're O.K. Have a good flight to New York, and tell your wife to call the office to make an appointment for a complete physical exam."

Ten days later, after I'd taken a history and completed the examination, Ruth helped Margaret off the examining table and said to her, "Get dressed and the doctor will talk to you in the consultation room."

While waiting, I racked my brain, trying to decide how I should tell her what was wrong; I didn't want to embarrass her by telling her that their intercourse had been anal, not vaginal. In a few minutes she walked into the room and promptly asked, "Can my husband come in, he's in the waiting room."

"Ruth is already on her way to show him in. Hello, George. Please sit down in the chair next to your wife."

"Did you find out what's wrong with my wife?"

"Yes, and it's nothing serious. Your wife has a very thick membrane that prohibits your sperm from entering the uterus. I can fix that, but it will have to be done in the hospital."

"Then we could have children?"

"Yes, of course. Margaret would be able to come home the same day she is operated, and you could resume sex three weeks later. It takes that long for the site to heal."

"Is this rare, what Margaret has?"

"Not at all, and I've never failed to correct it."

"When can you do the operation?"

"Ruth will discuss that with you. She'll call the hospital and get you the day and time of surgery. If you have any questions after you get home and relax, call me. I'll always answer as soon as I can."

The surgery consisted of removing the hymen by a cross-incision and excising the unusually tough, fibrous tissue. The minimal bleeding was easily controlled by simple cautery. Margaret's menstrual flows had been regular but scant since she was fourteen years old, exiting through a tiny hole at the top of her hymen. At no time had she been able to have vaginal coitus, but now she was cured.

Three months later she called and made an appointment. I found her to be four weeks pregnant. Eight months later she delivered a seven-pound, three-ounce boy with no difficulty or complication. I delivered her three times—two boys and one girl. She referred many a patient to me. Never was the "mistaken identity" mentioned or referred to, by her, him, or me.

Chapter 8

Self-delivery

It was eleven p.m. and I was preparing to go to bed when the phone rang.

"Doctor Parker?"

"Yes."

"This is Mrs. Exeter. You know me; you removed that big cyst from my ovary three months ago. I would like you to make a house call—it's very important."

"What is your problem?" I asked.

"It's not me, it's my daughter, Nancy. She just had a baby."

"That's nice. Is it Nancy or her baby who's ill?"

"*Please,* Doctor, come. It's very important; I can't say any more now."

"What's your address?"

She carefully gave me the street, the number, and directions. "Its only four miles above your office. I'll leave the porch light on." She hung up before I could ask any more questions. While driving up the steep and winding, single-lane gravel road, I kept wondering, *what's wrong with Nancy or her child, and why couldn't she tell me over the phone?* The nearer I got to my destination, the uneasier I became. *What am I getting myself into?*

The Exeter home's porch light illuminated a broad, flat piece of land. I parked my old Dodge and got out. Flashlight in one hand and medical bag in the other, I climbed an incline for 100 feet or more to a stairway one story tall and knocked on the front door.

"Come in, Doctor, follow me, Nancy is in the bedroom." There lay Nancy, on a huge bed, a newborn in her arms.

"Hello, Nancy, I'm Doctor Parker."

"Yeah, I know you."

"Are you in any pain?" I asked.

"No."

"And how is your baby?"

"She's fine."

"I'm pleased to hear that. Your baby sure looks pretty—you must be very proud. Tell me, when was she born, and at which hospital?"

Nancy said, "I borned her in the Mark movie theater on Colorado Street."

Stunned, I hardly knew what to say. After a pause, I continued, "Nancy, please tell me exactly what happened."

"Yeah, sure. Today, all afternoon I was having cramps in my belly. I knew I was pregnant but I wasn't sure what was happening. My girlfriend who has a baby told me I was due in June and this is only May. Tonight I went to work; my belly wasn't hurting as bad as before. Suddenly when I was ushering an old lady to her seat, a lot of water came spilling down my legs. I showed the old lady into her seat and hurried toward the ladies room, waving at my girlfriend, Florence, who was ushering on the next aisle, to come quickly and follow me. I told her, "Lock the door." I took off my pants and there was this tiny foot sticking out between my legs. I grabbed it and pulled, pretty hard. Out came both legs and feet. I pulled some more and more and even twisted the body back and forth, till suddenly out came the whole baby. I had to kneel down – I was tired – "

"Did the baby cry?" I interrupted.

"Yeah, right away. There was a rope connected to the baby's belly and the other end went up into my vagina. Florence said I should cut this thing, but we had no knife or scissors. So, I grabbed the rope between my vagina and the baby and squeezed it so tight that I was able to rip it in half by twisting and turning it. My girlfriend held the baby."

"What did you do with the rope that was hanging out of your vagina?"

"Oh, I just grabbed it and pulled till it popped out with a hunk of meat about the size of your fist."

"Did you bleed a lot?" I asked.

"My hands and feet were pretty bloody, but Florence handed me plenty of paper towels, so it wasn't too bad."

"What did you do next?" I asked unbelievingly.

"I flushed the rope and the attached meat down the toilet. Then I sat down on the toilet and took my baby from Florence. I told her to go get a taxi. The driver waited for us after Florence told him we were coming. I took the baby and told the driver to take us home. Florence didn't come—she stayed to clean up the toilet room floor."

I turned toward Nancy's mother, who hadn't uttered a word during this conversation, and asked, "Did Nancy tell you this same story?"

"Yes, exactly like she told you."

"Did you know she was pregnant?"

"No! Never!"

With a sigh of disbelief I asked, "How old is Nancy?"

"She'll be fifteen next week."

"Thank you. Nancy, I would now like to check you and your baby to make sure all is well, O.K.?"

"Sure, I want you to check everything."

I examined Nancy; she was fine and the baby was perfect—not a fault or blemish on her. "Nancy, I'm now going to tie the umbilical cord—the rope—and cut the excess length off. I want your mother to bring this wonderful baby to my office tomorrow morning, so I can weigh her, and especially so I can put some drops of medicine in her eyes. That's necessary to prevent infection, and is required by law. Do you understand?"

"Sure. Can I come along?"

"I'd rather you stay home and rest, but I'll return tomorrow and make sure you're well."

"O.K., Doc."

"Nancy, before I leave, I want to tell you what an unusually brave and wonderful lady you are. I'm glad you had your mother call me. I'll never forget you, and wish the best for you."

The next morning, Mrs. Exeter brought the baby to the office, as requested. She weighed five pounds, two ounces and was "fit as a fiddle." Later that day I checked Nancy at home. "All is well. You can move about the house tomorrow, but be sure to call me if you don't feel well or are bleeding more than a regular menstrual period. In two weeks come to my office with your baby."

"I'll do all you tell me to do. Thanks, Doc—I like you."

That was the last I heard from the family. When Nancy did not return in two weeks, I drove out to the house. It was empty, and the neighbors, a quarter mile away, didn't know when or where they'd moved.

Chapter 9

I Must Get Rid of This Pregnancy

It had been a busy week for me: six deliveries—five during the small hours of the night—a difficult hysterectomy, an ectopic pregnancy, and three minor surgeries, plus the usual crowded office hours and several house calls. Our small California town was in the grip of a terrible flu epidemic. People weren't dying, as in the flu epidemic of 1918, but they were very ill, running high fevers, and having uncontrollable fits of coughing that left them gasping for air. This was 1947, and penicillin was available. In many cases it made the difference between recovery and death. Without it we would have been ineffective in treating the bronchopneumonia that so frequently complicated flu. Our peers in 1918 had had no such weapon.

Our office was a compact and efficient two-story building at the very edge of town. We were almost completely engulfed by the Sierra Madre Mountains, except for several scattered residential homes and tiny farms. The senior member of our group, a general surgeon and owner of the building, was in his mid-fifties. We doctors knew him as "Serge" (short for "Sergeant"). A stubborn Dutchman, Serge was a master surgeon, and his devotion to work was boundless. During World War II, he single-handedly served this town of 10,000 people. On his staff were Art, the general practitioner, Rand, the internist and cardiologist, and me, the obstetrician and gynecologist. We three were fresh out of the army and all in our thirties.

This particular week our clinic was averaging forty house calls a day, almost all of them "flu" cases. In many of the homes we had to treat more than one patient—two to three on average. We all made house calls. There was no way any one person could handle them alone. Hospital emergency rooms existed, but without physicians present or on call. The "emergency specialist" doctor didn't exist. If you sent a patient to the emergency room, you were expected to be there to take care of him—there was no passing the buck. I was exhausted at the end of this week, and went to bed near midnight. I was awakened from a sound sleep by the ringing of my bedside phone. Before I could say "Hello," I heard, "I h-h—hate to b-b-bother you at home, d-d-doctor, and I h-h-hope I d-d—din't wake you, but I-I-I-I'm so worried... I'm pregnant."

"Who is this?" I asked.

"M-M-Marion Cook."

"Look, Marion, take a slow, deep breath, now let it out. That's good, now do it again, slow and deep, now blow it out. All right, now tell me what happened."

"I have this gentleman friend. We enjoy each other's company. He is always a gentleman, Doctor. We go out to eat a lot. He always takes me to the best places—you know, like Romanoff's or Scandia— "

"Yes, Marion," I interrupted, "I understand, you had intercourse."

"Oh, no, Doctor! You don't understand, we like each other... but we never did that... well not unless, maybe for a second, he might have. I'm not sure. Oh, God! He is such a gentleman."

"You have nothing to worry about," I tried to reassure her. "Please go to bed and call me in the morning at the office."

"Oh, no, Doctor, I can't! I know a personal friend who got pregnant when she was fifty-eight years old, and I'm only fifty-five. I think she was from Italy somewhere. I read it in the paper last year."

"Marion, please relax, you can't be pregnant."

"I didn't use anything to prevent pregnancy, except now, I have large ice cubes in my vah-jean-ah."

"You what?" I said.

"Yah, I put ice cubes in my vah-jean-ah, because I read in the magazine once that cold freezes sperm stiff."

"Marion, listen. Take the ice cubes out of your vagina right now."

"I can't, Doctor. I tried. They won't come out, they're too big."

"O.K., listen. Fill your bathtub with warm water, good and warm, but don't burn yourself. Then get in the tub and the ice cubes will melt some and then you should easily be able to get them out of your vagina with your fingers."

"But, Doctor, I'm afraid to take them out, the sperm may move."

"No, they won't. The hot water will kill them."

"But, Doctor, don't you think you should come over and do something. I'm sure I'm pregnant."

"Marion, do as I say, then come to the office in the morning. I promise I won't let you be pregnant." I hung up the phone. She didn't call back, but was in my office when I arrived in the morning. My records showed that Marion was fifty-seven years old and had not had a menstrual period for eight years. There was no way she could be pregnant, but I couldn't convince her. I greeted her courteously and asked my nurse to prepare her for a pelvic examination. During the procedure, I repeatedly reassured Marion that there were absolutely no signs of pregnancy, but to be positively and 100 percent sure, I would now treat her entire vagina with a solution no pregnancy could survive. I proceeded to paint her entire vagina and external genitalia with an innocuous deep-staining gentian violet solution. "There, now," I said, "you can't possibly be pregnant." She thanked me profusely. For many years Marion referred patients to me, and every Christmas I received a wonderful card graced with thanks. She died of a stroke at seventy.

Chapter 10

An Indian Squats

"Good morning, Doctor."

"Good morning, Ruth," I answered.

"Before you go into your consultation room, Doctor, please let me explain that an American-Indian man is sitting in the waiting room. He has long hair, and is well dressed, very courteous, and handsome. He insists on talking to you before you see any patients; he promised he would only take a few minutes. It's about his pregnant wife, who insisted on staying at home."

"I'll talk to him, Ruth. Show him to my room while I make a phone call." Having completed the call, I walked down the hall and opened the door to my consultation room. "Hello, sir, what can I do for you?" He got up from the chair, shook my hand manfully, and said, "Doctor, I want you to deliver my wife."

"Well, thank you," I responded. "Why don't you make an appointment at the front office for her. I'll be happy to examine her in the office and deliver her at either of the hospitals in town."

"That's why I'm here, Doctor—she doesn't want any examinations, and insists on having her baby at home."

"I'm sorry, but I do no deliveries at home."

"I'll pay you now if you'll come to the house."

"It's not the money, it's just that I can't deliver the baby at home."

"O.K., Doctor. My name is Jim Longstick. I'm happy to have met and talked with you. Now I'll go home and tell my wife. Thank you very much."

"I sincerely hope you can talk your wife into changing her mind about coming here." He left immediately after first giving me another emphatic handshake.

Three months later, my phone rang at two a.m.

"Doctor Parker?"

"Yes, who is this?"

"I'm Ellen, at St. Luke's delivery room. We have a woman who came in and she says she's your patient."

"What's her name?" I asked.

"Mrs. Longstick. I think she is an Indian."

"No kidding, Longstick—oh, yes, I remember, I saw her husband a few months ago. He told me she wanted a home delivery. I never saw her. How far along is she in labor?"

"I don't know; she won't let me examine her. She won't even get into bed, and is squatting in the corner of the delivery room. What should I do?"

"Do nothing. I'll be there in fifteen minutes." When I arrived at the hospital, there she was, squatting in the corner of the room. "Hello, Mrs. Longstick. I'm Doctor Parker. How are you?"

"Fine," she grunted softly.

"Good, let's get you on the bed," I said.

"No, no. I'm fine. I think the baby is coming soon—just wait, please wait."

I turned to the nurse and said, "Ellen, get a pillow off the bed and shove it under her buttocks, so the baby has a soft landing. I'll be right back. I want to change into my scrub suit."

A few minutes later, Sister Liguori, the chief of the hospital, stormed in. "Doctor Parker, you can't let this woman labor on the floor—let's get her onto the bed."

"She won't go," I replied.

"Then we'll put her on the bed whether she wants to or not—let's go."

I didn't budge.

"Let's go," Sister Liguori repeated and added, "If anything happens to her or the baby, you, Doctor Parker, and the hospital, will be responsible for allowing her to squat."

"Please, Sister Liguori, don't be concerned. I will not leave her alone, not even for a minute. I'll take full blame if anything happens." Useless and increasingly threatening remarks continued between Sister Liguori and me for a good fifteen minutes. Then, like a bolt of lightning, it all climaxed with a loud, prolonged and victorious grunt. Out popped the baby onto the pillow where nurse Ellen had placed it. With my gloved hands I scooped the baby off the pillow and cleared its throat with a bulb syringe that the nurse handed me. Immediately, the baby gave out a vigorous, healthy scream. While still on my knees beside the squatting woman, I clamped the cord with the clamps Ellen handed me. I cut the cord and handed the baby to his mother. "It's a boy, Mrs. Longstick, healthy and beautiful. I want to congratulate you. Your delivery was perfect. I'll never forget it."

"Thank you, Doctor, thank you." Willingly, the woman allowed Ellen, Sister Liguori, and me to get her onto the bed alongside which she had squatted. Ellen then covered her with a sheet and blanket, and placed the baby boy in his mother's arms. She became so absorbed with cuddling her son that she offered no resistance when I told her I had to remove the afterbirth and inspect her vagina to make sure there were no lacerations. This was accomplished with ease. The placenta delivered without difficulty and was normal. The vagina was intact. "All is well, Mrs. Longstick. Now I'm going to talk to your husband and give him the good news."

"Thank you, thank you, Doctor," was all she could say.

As I started toward the waiting room, Sister Liguori intercepted me. "Doctor Parker, I want you to know that you were right in allowing Mrs. Longstick to remain squatting during her labor, and I hope you understand that, as chief of this hospital, I had to stick to the rules and continue to warn you."

"Thanks, Sister Liguori. I know it was difficult for you to do. I believe that Mrs. Longstick was only exercising her inborn sense of what was right. We must all learn to trust our own consciences, just as we learn to trust our own eyes and actions."

Sister Liguori and I remained the best of friends.

As I continued alone toward the expectant father's room, an anxious Jim Longstick met me at the doorway. "Is Maria alright? I am so worried," he asked.

"She's just fine, and you have a healthy and well-built son."

"Can I see them now?"

"In a few minutes, Jim. The nurse is changing Maria's clothes and then she and your son will be moved to a room where you can see and hold them both." We were alone in the waiting room so I asked him, "Please tell me how you were able to get Maria to the hospital. I know she didn't want to come here."

"Maria had made arrangements for some lady to come to our house when labor started."

"Is this lady, whatever her name is, a doctor or midwife?"

"I don't know. Her name is Julia. She stayed with Maria for over sixteen hours. All this time Maria was hurting a lot and grunted a lot. After sixteen hours, Julia told me that she had to leave, because she was wanted at another house where a woman was also in labor. Besides, she said, 'Maria's problem delivering the baby has to be corrected by a doctor in the hospital. You must take her to the hospital *now*,' she emphasized. She put on her hat and coat and left right away. Maria and I were left alone. When I said, 'I'm taking you to the hospital now,' she screamed, 'No, no, I won't go.'

"I couldn't stand it any longer, so I slapped Maria across the face, very hard, picked her up—bed sheets and all—and put her in the car. On our way I told her several times to keep still. Poor thing, she was so scared. Believe me, Doctor, I never hit her before. As soon as we got to the hospital, I held her real hard and walked her directly to the delivery area. The nurse at the entrance made me let go of her and told me to go to the front office—she didn't let me kiss Maria. That's about all, Doctor."

"It's all over now, Jim. You did nothing wrong, and I'm sure your wife, Maria, understands and will welcome you with open arms."

"Thank you, Doctor, thank you so much. You must be especially good. Maria labored at home for over sixteen hours and nothing happened, yet in less than one hour you fixed her problem and delivered her. Did you have to do a big operation to get the baby?"

"No, Jim, I did nothing. Maria delivered herself by squatting by her bed in the corner of the labor room."

"Squatting, what is that?" implored Jim.

"It means a woman bends her knees and gets in a sitting position so her ass rests on or near her heels. She stays in this position then pushes hard with each labor pain. If the baby doesn't pop out after a few labor pains, the doctor must take over to solve the problem. The woman is put to sleep and the doctor applies special instruments, called forceps, to reposition the baby's head. If this is unsuccessful, a Caesarian delivery must be done."

"How come the lady at home made Maria stay in bed? I heard Maria beg her to get out of bed and let her sit on her ass."

"I don't know," I replied. Jim was completely satisfied with my explanation, and asked no more. Maria and baby went home after two days' rest in the hospital. My bill and the hospital bill were paid promptly and in full. I never saw the Longsticks again. Their neighbors told me that they moved back to Arizona just a week after the baby was born.

When I got home, that memorable night, I recalled clearly having seen a movie a long time ago in which a Chinese woman squatted in a rice paddy, delivered her baby, handed it to a friend, and then continued to work in the paddy.

Squatting makes it easier for the baby coming headfirst to progress through the vagina after the cervix has completely dilated (opened). The squat also allows the baby to put its chin to its chest, which makes the diameter of the oncoming head smaller, allowing it to slide through the vagina with ease.

Many doctors now allow patients in labor to squat after the cervix has completely dilated, if they wish to. Some hospitals even have delivery tables that convert to allow the patient to squat and labor after the cervix is fully dilated. I helped Mrs. Longstick deliver her baby in 1949. An article that appeared in the January 2003 issue of *Southern California Physician* noted that squatting was the preferred method of delivery in the ancient world, and remains the method of choice in many non-Western cultures. The squatting position, which, in a woman lying on her back, can be simulated by pushing her knees into her chest and applying pressure to her feet, widens the opening of the pelvis and allows gravity to assist the woman's efforts at pushing. Many physicians feel that there's no drawback to squatting, while some difficulties can arise from delivering while lying on one's back.

"It is much easier to be critical than to be correct."
—Benjamin Disraeli

Chapter 11

Post Squatting

I almost always enter my office through the back door, as it avoids going through the waiting room. I did so this day. "Good morning, Ruth."

"Good morning, Doctor. Ellen, the night nurse from St. Luke's Hospital, is in your consulting room. She wants to talk to you for just a few minutes."

"Fine, I'll see her now." I changed into my white coat before entering the room. "Hi, Ellen, it's nice to see you—please don't get up—what can I do for you?"

"Thanks for seeing me right away, Doctor Parker. I'm three months pregnant, but I didn't want to make an appointment as a new patient of yours until I could ask you a question or two in private."

"Very good, please do," I responded.

"As you know, I have two girls, and Doctor Lanier was my

obstetrician for both. With my first labor, after my cervix was completely dilated, Doctor Lanier was summoned to the hospital across town to control a severe bleeding patient whose placenta had separated. Doctor Lanier explained to me why he had to leave me immediately, and said that his partner, Doctor Singer, would arrive very soon to stay with me and deliver me if necessary. For some reason, Doctor Singer didn't arrive, and I labored alone for almost two hours.

"The nurse on duty wanted to inject Demerol, the pain-killer that Doctor Lanier had left orders for, but I refused it. Instead, each time she left my room I would squat in bed and push with the next contraction, over and over, until finally I delivered in bed, alone and with no difficulty. I felt absolutely exhausted but ever so gratified. There were no complications.

"Two years later I went back to Doctor Lanier for my second pregnancy. During this labor I again refused the pain medication he'd prescribed. The labor progressed normally and Doctor Lanier examined me regularly. I'd been in the hospital less than four hours when, without notice, I was put on a cart and wheeled into the delivery room. Doctor Lanier was standing in the corner, wrapped in a sterile gown, with his gloved hands upright like a boxer ready to fight. He said he was going to give me a spinal injection. When I asked why, he said it was because my cervix had been dilated completely for more than a half hour, and the baby's head was unable to descend through the vagina. He needed to give me a spinal so he could use forceps to turn the baby's head in the correct direction so it could be born.

"'Doctor,' I said, 'can't you wait? Remember I told you that with the last delivery it took over two hours after the cervix was completely dilated for the baby to be born. Please wait—I don't want a spinal.'

"With an ostentatious display of authority, he pronounced that he must deliver now or severe damage could result to the baby. 'I won't give you a spinal, but I'll inject Novocain locally to get it done.' He went ahead, and all went well, but I will never go back to him again."

"I understand your point, Ellen, but you and I both know Doctor Lanier is an excellent obstetrician—he can be abrupt, but we all have our faults. Can I ask why you want me to deliver you?"

After hesitating, Ellen said, "Last month I helped you with Mrs. Longstick's delivery. I especially liked it when you stood firm and said no to Sister Liguori when she kept insisting that you make Mrs. Longstick stop squatting and get into bed. I want you to promise that you'll allow me to labor without painkillers, and leave me alone even if it takes two hours or longer to deliver after my cervix has completely dilated. I might want to squat, but I'll do it in bed."

"Ellen, I don't fully comprehend why you want to have your labor this way, but I'll promise to do as you ask. However, if a condition arises that puts you or the baby in jeopardy, I'll first explain it to you fully before I interfere in any way."

"Thank you, Doctor Parker, I'll make my appointment with you now."

Six Months Later:

"Ellen, you're doing just fine; your cervix is already halfway dilated. I'll be in the doctors' waiting room down the hall. Call if you need anything. Otherwise, I'll recheck your cervix in about a half hour."

"Thank you, Doctor, I'll be fine," she responded with a smile.

I went next to the expectant fathers' room, which was just beyond the doctor's waiting room. Back in those days, fathers were not allowed in the labor rooms. "Ellen is doing great—I'll keep you fully informed as she progresses. Do you have any questions?" I asked.

"Not really, except, when will she deliver?"

"I would presume in the next two to three hours," I replied, with my fingers crossed behind me. "You can turn on the TV, or you can browse through the magazines and books to your left side."

"Thanks, Doc," he said.

A Half Hour Later:

"Ellen, your cervix is completely dilated now. I'll go back to the doctor's room; call if you want anything. I'll return every once in a while to check your progress."

"Thanks, Doc. I'll tell you when I want you to stay, 'cause I'll know when I'm going to deliver, and I want to do it in bed."

Very slowly, the baby was coming headfirst through the tunnel-like passageway of the vagina. Each time I examined Ellen I found the baby's head in an *occiput posterior* position, meaning the baby was looking up toward the sky instead of bowing its head and looking toward the ground. If Ellen would allow me to turn the baby's head with forceps, the diameter of the oncoming head would be much less, and its passage through the vagina could be accomplished safely in less than five minutes, but I had promised, so I didn't interfere.

The vital signs remained normal in both mom and baby. With each contraction of the uterus, Ellen would suck air slowly, yet progressively deeper, into her lungs, and then exhale slowly with a barely audible sigh. This went on for over an hour and a half. Her expression wasn't one of pain or apprehension; in fact, it resembled accomplishment and satisfaction. Her forehead was covered with beads of perspiration. Then, her sucking-like inspirations suddenly became louder. By chance, I was in the labor room as it happened.

"The baby is coming *now,*" she cried out. "Stay here, now, Doc, stay here, please—it's coming."

The boy was born in bed following the third contraction.

"Oh, I'm so spent, but I'm so happy and so thankful that you let me do it my way. Thank you, Doctor Parker, thank you."

Three Weeks Later

"Doctor Parker, Ellen is in your consultation room; she wants to talk to you."

"O.K., I'll see her now."

As I opened the door, Ellen got up from the chair and said,

"Doctor, I probably won't see you again. We're moving soon to Finland, where my husband, Karl, was born. He was offered a promotion he couldn't refuse—the salary starts at three times what he's making here. We'll probably make our home there forever. I really love Karl. No one could have a better husband. I could never tell him I don't want to live in Finland. Before we leave, I wanted to thank you for allowing me to deliver my way."

"They'll miss you very much at the hospital. You're one of the best nurses they ever had. And I want to wish you the best in Finland. I'm sure you'll grow to like it. It's cold and wet a lot, but very beautiful, and the people are most friendly."

Ellen got up and headed for the door.

I said, "I'd like to ask you a question or two, Ellen; please sit down again." She did.

"Why were you so insistent on not having any medication during your labor?"

She hesitated for some time; then, with tears in her eyes she began. "Doctor, I've never told anyone, not even my husband, but I will never forget what happened with my first labor. I'm so ashamed, but I just have to tell you. I had my first... orgasm. I've never forgotten the climax and the emotional excitement I experienced. As you know, with my second labor, Doctor Lanier insisted on giving me medication and using forceps to turn the baby's head. I never forgave him. Thank God, you let me do what I did—it was just as successful as the first time. I want to thank you again, most sincerely."

I was stunned, and before I could utter a word, she was up from her chair and headed toward the door. "Just a minute, Ellen, please. I want to tell you that you mustn't be ashamed. You did nothing wrong or abnormal. Many women have never experienced orgasm. I've had several patients who have told me this. You say you love your husband and think he's the best. I feel it would be best if you told him what you just told me. I'm sure he'll understand and will help you. But, if you don't want to tell him, then be sure to discuss this matter with a knowledgeable doctor in Finland. It's important you get help, or you might end up getting severely hurt."

"Thanks, Doctor. I'm so relieved that I told you, and I will talk to my husband."

I never saw or heard from Ellen again.

Chapter 12

Summation

This very long and busy day began at my office at nine a.m. My first patient was Ellen, the obstetrical nurse who delivered herself at the hospital, in my presence, six weeks ago. She was in for her six-week check and was leaving for Finland in three days. After her, I saw twenty more patients, interrupted by the delivery of a baby girl at the hospital. Some patients were rescheduled, but most waited until I returned from the hospital, at least an hour later.

After getting home late for dinner, I had to stop eating and rush to the hospital to do an emergency Caesarian section. The ambulance had brought in a woman in labor and hemorrhaging. She had no doctor, so the nurse called me, because I was the obstetrician on call today for all obstetrical emergencies who had no private physician.

Luckily, there was another patient in labor, and her doctor was there. The obstetrical nurse asked him to examine the unknown woman; at once he diagnosed that she had a *placenta previa,* which means the afterbirth was separating and attempting to deliver before the child. He immediately called surgery and the laboratory to prepare for a Caesarian operation. Unhesitatingly, this obstetrician volunteered to be my assistant at that operation. I wasted no time in delivering the baby by Caesarian, as mother and her baby were at death's door. Both did fine. No transfusions were needed, but the blood had been typed and readied for use. Neither the hospital, nor the ambulance service, nor we doctors ever billed this patient: we all knew she was poor and needed help. That's the way it was in 1957. No one complained; we all took our turn in caring for the poor and needy.

It was midnight when I finally flopped into my comfortable chair at home and slowly drank a tall, cold Pepsi. Mable had already retired, but as always, she left me a note instructing me how to warm the food to complete my dinner. "She never forgets me. Thank you, God," I said in the empty room, "for giving her to me."

Yes, I was not only busy today but also deeply affected by Ellen's confession. Unable to stop musing about her revelation, I suddenly remembered something that had happened in 1947 when I first started practicing medicine. Katherine was a beautiful twenty-five-year-old girl who had been married three years and had no children. Four Mondays in a row she came to my office with evident injuries: once a black eye, the other times, black-and-blue areas on her breast, arms, and abdomen. The last time, I had to suture two superficial cuts on her face. It was always Monday when she came to the office. I finally asked her, "Does your husband beat you up, and why?"

She was very hesitant; then, with tears flowing down her cheeks, she very quietly said, "No, it's not my husband. He's been gone every weekend for the last four months, working in Lancaster, so I've been all alone. Then, I found a place in Los Angeles where, every weekend, I got pleasure that I never thought possible. That's why I always come to you on Monday to heal my wounds."

We talked for quite a long time, but I was incapable of coming up with a satisfactory solution to her dilemma, so I closed the conversation by saying, "Katherine, you must see a psychiatrist for your own safety." She agreed. I made sure the appointment was made and carried out.

Two months later, while eating breakfast and reading our local newspaper, I was stunned to see: Katherine Williams found dead at home by hanging. I couldn't believe it. Without hesitation I called the psychiatrist at his home, inadvertently waking him—it was seven a.m. I told him what I had just read in the newspaper. He coughed a couple of times and then replied, "Oh, yeah, I know Katherine. I saw her three or four times and told her that her problem was her tiny breasts, because of which she wanted to prove to herself that men really loved her. I strongly suggested she see a plastic surgeon I know, and assured her that he could operate and make her breasts full and lovable. She agreed, but never saw him—if she had done what I told her to do, she would never have killed herself."

In disbelief I thanked the psychiatrist for his information, and never again referred a patient to him. The psychiatrist had misdiagnosed Katherine—and so had I.

Both Ellen and Katherine had been my patients; both had the same condition, and I didn't recognize it. They suffered from masochism, a sexual deviation characterized by intense pleasure in being abused during lovemaking. Katherine knew her problem well. She felt I shunned her when I referred her to a psychiatrist. He in turn was absolutely wrong when he told her that small breasts were the cause of her predicament. Feeling she had no one to help her, she committed suicide.

I hope tomorrow is a better day.

Chapter 13
Laughter

We are the only animals that laugh. Why do we do it? It makes us feel good; we enjoy hearing a funny joke, though some have sharp edges and can hurt deeply—ethnic jokes, for example, deride and ridicule a specific person or class. Why do we repeat them? Could it be that we like to demonstrate our superiority over the butt of the joke?

I know that laughter is usually good medicine. A hearty laugh relaxes the body, speeds up the heart, and increases oxygen supply to the brain and muscles. It can release endorphins, the body's natural painkillers. Too often we worry too much. It's time to relax then, put aside the work we've slaved at, and just rear back and laugh at nothing in particular just because it feels so good. How about going to a funny movie or renting a hilarious videotape? It makes no difference if it's new or if you've seen it many times, just so it makes you laugh. Try it—it works.

I'll tell you some jokes, because that's what I feel like doing today. Enjoy.

A man consulted a marriage counselor concerning his wife's sexual indifference. The counselor suggested that he be more aggressive in his lovemaking. "When you go home, grab her, caress her, make love to her as soon as you're with her... even if it's right inside the front door."

At the next consultation, the counselor was pleased to hear that the husband was following instructions. "And how did she react this time?"

"Well," answered the husband, "she wasn't much different—but her bridge group went absolutely wild!"

An attractive young schoolteacher saved enough money for a romantic ocean cruise. Aboard ship, she kept a diary of her adventures.

"Monday: Dear Diary, I was very honored this evening when the captain asked me to dine at his table. He was very attentive.
Tuesday: I spent the entire morning on the bridge with the captain. He was very friendly.
Wednesday: The captain made proposals that were unbecoming to an officer and a gentleman.
Thursday: Tonight the captain threatened to sink the ship if I didn't give in to his indecent proposals.
Friday: This afternoon I saved 1,600 lives."

Laughter has many faces. Though mostly for fun, it can be used to resolve a seemingly insoluble muddle. Abraham Lincoln was a witty and celebrated storyteller. He was also a worrier and chronically depressed man, but he knew how to break an impasse. A crucial meeting with his cabinet on how to continue the Civil War, which appeared headed toward defeat, was deadlocked. Lincoln, pokerfaced, asked an irrelevant and unexpected question: "What I would like to know is, who dislikes strawberries?" Then he farted out loud. All the cabinet members erupted in laughter. The president had broken the tension. The meeting resumed on a much more productive level. My grandfather told me this story, and swore it was true.

The average woman would rather have beauty than brains because she knows that the average man can see better than he can think.

A visitor to America says, "Funny people, you Americans: You take a glass, put in sugar to make it sweet, and lemon to make it sour; you put in gin to warm you up, and ice to keep you cool. You say, 'Here's to you' and then you drink it yourself."

When Bill, an intern at a local hospital, got married, he asked for a two-week vacation to go to Mexico on his honeymoon. After the two weeks were up, he wired the hospital, "Please extend vacation two more weeks. It's wonderful here." His boss wired back: "Return at once—it's wonderful anywhere."

A physician picking up his car at a garage was amazed by the size of the repair bill. After he recovered from his surprise, he commented casually to the mechanic, "You fellows charge more for your work than we in the medical profession do." "Well," said the mechanic, "we deserve it. You fellows have been working on the same old model since time began, but we have to learn a new one every year."

After grace had been said at the dinner table, a little boy was told to leave and wash his hands, because they were filthy. As he got up, he muttered, "Jesus and germs, Jesus and germs. That's all I ever hear about and I've never seen either of them."

The lion ate a bull. He felt so good that he roared and roared. The hunter heard him and killed the lion. The moral of the story: When you're full of bull, keep your mouth shut.

Chapter 14

Acute Abdomen

B*rrring ... Brrring ... Brring–*

"Hello, Doctor Parker?"

"Yes."

"Doctor, this is Mr. Vanderhoff. Could you come over right away?"

"What's the problem?"

"It's my wife, she is in terrible pain–listen, you can hear her."

"I hear, what hurts her?"

"It's her stomach, it's awful. Please come right away."

"Give me your address; I'll be right over."

I hung up the phone. My wife woke up and asked if she could fix me some breakfast.

"No, thanks, honey, I've got to run. I'll be back later to eat;

please try to go back to sleep, it's only five a.m."

On my way to the Vanderhoffs', I thought about what condition might cause an acute abdomen that produced pain severe enough to make Mrs. Vanderhoff scream. Certainly an attack of acute appendicitis wouldn't, but a sudden rupture or twisting of the bowel could. She might be passing a stone from her kidney or gall bladder—*that* hurts. Even the most stoic has been known to scream when passing a stone. She could have twisted an ovarian cyst—very painful. Maybe they had a fight and Mr. Vanderhoff punched her in the belly.

It was only a ten-minute drive to their home. Mr. Vanderhoff was standing on the porch as I drove up. The porch light was on, as were all the lights inside.

"Quickly," he said, "come into the bedroom."

I ran up the porch steps, through the living room, and into the bedroom.

Mrs. Vanderhoff was in bed, lying on her back, her forehead covered with beads of sweat, and a blanket pulled up to her chin. She was breathing more rapidly than normal but didn't appear in pain.

"Hello. Mrs. Vanderhoff, I'm Doctor Parker. Please show me where it hurts."

She placed her hand on her abdomen, which was still covered with the blanket. "All over here," she said, rubbing her hand over the entire abdomen. As I turned to open my bag, she suddenly let out a bloodcurdling scream—I'm sure it could be heard next door. She didn't stop for over a minute, which seemed like an eternity. I turned down the blanket and pulled up her nightgown. Her belly was distended. Mrs. Vanderhoff was an enormous woman—over 300 pounds, I guessed. It was difficult to palpate her belly through the thick layer of fat, but as I did, I felt more and more sure that I was feeling a large oval mass, the size of a bucket, which I could move a bit from side to side. I pressed my hand deeper into her belly, and felt with the tip of my fingers what I was almost certain seemed to be *a body.* I looked up at her quizzically but didn't utter a word. She responded with a smile that would soften the heart of a grump. I took out my stethoscope, placed it on her belly, and began searching for the telltale heartbeat; I couldn't hear it—there was too much fatty insulation to transmit a sound. I put on sterile gloves and asked Mrs. Vanderhoff to bend her knees and bring up her feet. I spread her legs with my elbows so as not to contaminate the gloves, and inserted the fingers of my right hand into her vagina—or tried to. I was barely able to insert the tip of my fingers when I ran into an obvious barrier—the baby's head. I could feel no cervix—she was fully dilated—and was surely going to deliver with the next pain. I yelled for her husband who was waiting anxiously in the living room.

"Get me some clean towels and a basin and boil some water. *Hurry!*"

He disappeared without question. Mrs. Vanderhoff let out another scream.

"Take it easy, don't push," I cried. Gently, I guided the baby's head over the perineum, and the rest of its body literally shot out of her. I raised the infant by the feet, holding her upside down to let the mucus drain out of the nose and throat. She cried at once.

"Mrs. Vanderhoff, you're a mother. Congratulations—it's a girl!" At the same time, Mr. Vanderhoff was back with a pot of hot water and towels.

"What happened?"

"You're a father. Congratulations!"

"You mean she had a baby?" he asked.

"Yes, she did, and don't tell me you didn't know."

"I had no idea. God! Is that wonderful? You hear that, Eileen? I got a baby."

"Yeah, Bill, I know. I'm holding her." With tears of happiness she handed the baby to Bill. He rubbed his cheek against the child. "She's so beautiful just like you—we'll call her Eileen."

While this was going on I tied and cut the umbilical cord, then examined Eileen, put antiseptic drops in the baby's eyes, counted her fingers and toes, flexed and extended her limbs, and measured her legs to be sure they were equal. If they're not equal in length, it usually means the child has a dislocated hip—early treatment with a splint can avoid a major operation later.

"Eileen, Bill, you have a healthy, normal, and beautiful girl." Just then Mrs. Vanderhoff jerked, her eyes opened wide, she almost yelled, but instead said, "What's that pain in my belly?"

"Everything is fine, Eileen, you're just passing the afterbirth; it'll only take a minute or two." With the next pain the placenta was expressed intact. Its cord had the normal three vessels—when there are only two, a defect in the newborn will almost always appear in the near future.

"Eileen, let's put the baby to your breast. I'm sure she's hungry, and you need some rest. Bill, how about making some coffee for us?"

He and I went into the kitchen.

"Bill, you really didn't know that your wife was in labor when you called me?"

"No, honestly I didn't."

"Come on, you just wanted to save the cost of hospitalization—?"

"No, I didn't know anything, believe me."

"How long have you two been married?"

"Over five years."

"Has Eileen always been this heavy?"

"I guess so, I never noticed," he said.

"Didn't she tell you that she hadn't menstruated for months?"

"No, I don't think so. In fact, I don't think she ever menstruated. I remember now—she said the last time she had a period was at her high school graduation. She said it was unexpected; she ruined her dress and had to go home early."

"Hmm. Why didn't you take her to the doctor—didn't you think that was unusual?"

"Well, Doc, she never complains and she always looks good. She works hard—you should see the garden she has in the backyard—would you like some corn? It's ripe and good now."

"Thank you, but not now. I'll look in on you all later today. I'll bring a scale so we can weigh your daughter; then, if it's convenient for you, pick me some corn. I'm sure I'll enjoy it."

During our chat, Bill had unobtrusively set the table for two, scrambled fresh eggs, fried thick slices of bacon, and poured hot coffee. The aroma was heavenly. We sat down and ate.

"Bill, you're a terrific cook, I've never enjoyed a breakfast more. This blackberry jam is the best I've ever tasted."

"Here, let me give you a few jars to take home. I'm sure your wife and children will like it too. Eileen made it."

"Bill, you're much too generous."

"It's nothing. Someday you must come and eat one of Eileen's dinners—that's *real* cooking!"

"I'd love to, thanks a million. I'll look in on Eileen now, and then I must get going. Thanks again, Bill."

Eileen was still awake, her eyes fixed admiringly on her daughter, who was sound asleep with her mother's nipple halfway out of her mouth.

"How are you feeling now, Eileen?"

"Just wonderful, Doctor—thank you so much."

"You're welcome; I'm glad everything turned out so well for you. Eileen, before I go I'd like to ask you a question."

"Sure, Doctor—anything."

"Eileen, did you know you were pregnant?"

"No, honestly, I didn't."

"You didn't feel the baby move in the past few months?"

"No, never, but I did notice something like gas pains once in a while. It concerned me, but I didn't tell Bill. It would only worry him, and he has enough worries at the shop. It's hard to get good workers today; he has to do most of the machine work himself. The aircraft companies are always in a hurry to get the parts he makes—you know he makes the best in the world. Even Mr. Martin, his boss from Lockheed, told me so."

Driving home, I was engulfed in waves of remorse. Why did I have to talk down to these two wonderful people? Why couldn't I have accepted without suspicion what they told me? No, I had to display my know-it-all attitude in its worst form. How I wished I'd kept my mouth shut; I wouldn't have needed to feel so bad. They came to my office for the next two pregnancies: I delivered one girl and one boy, both in the hospital, but never was it as much fun—it lacked the exhilaration of the home delivery.

Chapter 15

Dogs and Toxocariasis

Some time ago, while walking across my lawn, I inadvertently stepped into a heap of "recycled" dog food. Slipping and falling, I pulled my lower back and sprained my right wrist. My humiliation and discomfort were bad enough, but soon it turned to downright rage, and I dread to think what I might have done in retribution had I found the dog's owner. However, after cleaning up and cooling off, I decided that, instead of seeking revenge, I would turn my efforts to finding a solution to this ever increasing problem.

So, I combed the medical libraries, talked to veterinarians, consulted with my medical colleagues, and came up with some interesting facts. I discovered that the dog population in the United States is rapidly approaching the 100 million mark. The majority of them are concentrated in the cities, and each one contributes a daily supply of feces, most of which is never picked up. The pollution that has resulted is deplorable.

If you don't believe we have a problem, try taking a walk in your neighborhood, in the park, or on the beach. Some of those areas resemble minefields. If you're not careful where you step, you're sure to get messed up, and if you slip, you can get hurt. My accident wasn't unique; many people have been injured. Clinics and emergency rooms throughout the country have compiled records of people who've broken bones, sprained backs, and even fractured skulls in falls caused by slipping on dog feces.

Now, as disabling as these injuries can be, and as obnoxious and degrading as this pollution is, yet a more serious problem has arisen from these dog droppings—a disease known as toxocariasis. Most people, including some doctors, have probably never heard of toxocariasis. It's a parasitic infection in humans that is acquired from dogs and cats that have roundworms.

Veterinarians report that 50 percent of all puppies and over 25 percent of adult dogs have roundworms. These worms are forever laying eggs, and these eggs are discharged with the dogs' feces. The eggs have been shown to remain viable in the ground for years, even after exposure to extreme variations in temperature. We are put in jeopardy when we pick up sand or soil that contains the parasite's eggs. It's then that we can unknowingly ingest the eggs if we fail to wash our hands before smoking or handling food. In fact, we don't need to handle the contaminated soil; if we happen to be picnicking in the right spot, strong winds will deposit the eggs on our food for us. Children are especially susceptible, because they love to put their fingers in their mouths while playing in sand or dirt. When the eggs are swallowed, they hatch in the intestines. An immature form of the worm, called a larva, is born. The larvae then penetrate the intestinal wall and get into the blood and lymph streams, where they're free to travel all over the body.

In humans the larvae don't complete their development into roundworms as they do in dogs and cats. They remain as larvae, but can do a lot of damage nonetheless. If they lodge in the liver, they can cause it to enlarge and malfunction. If they get stuck in the lungs, they can cause a type of recurrent pneumonia. In the eyes they can cause blindness, in the brain a type of encephalitis, and in the heart they've been known to cause muscle damage. The larvae have a predilection for the eye, liver, and lung, but no organ is immune to their attack.

Two London physicians, Drs. Woodruff and Ashton, reported the case of a five-year-old boy who had an eye removed for a suspected retinoblastoma, a type of cancer of the eye. When the hospital pathologist examined the tumor, he had considerable difficulty identifying the granulomatous growth. It wasn't until he had made some 100 sections of the tumor that he found the toxocaral larva that caused the growth.

The *Journal of Clinical Pediatrics* presented a case report of a three-and-a-half-year-old boy who was admitted to the hospital because the attending physician couldn't diagnose the disease. The child had swollen glands in his neck, armpits, and groin, varying in size from that of a pea to a cherry. His spleen and liver were enlarged, and were easily felt by pressing on his belly. For two months he'd had a recurring fever and bouts of vomiting, and had become progressively weaker. He didn't want to play or eat and had lost considerable weight. The admitting diagnosis was possible Hodgkin's disease or leukemia. It took a week to make the correct diagnosis of toxocariasis. After instituting appropriate treatment, he recovered; when seen two months later, he was well. Liver and spleen had returned to normal size, and all the swollen glands had completely resolved.

A fifty-year-old man went to his doctor complaining of tiredness, loss of appetite, and night sweats of three days' duration. After examining him, the doctor assured the man that he had found nothing wrong and that it was probably some type of flu. He told him to rest, take aspirin, and report any worsening of his condition. Twenty-four hours later, the patient noted blurred vision and a distortion of images in his right eye, accompanied by pain in his face and scalp on the same side. He called the doctor, who had him admitted to the hospital. In the course of taking a complete history, the patient stated that he had found a stray puppy about eight weeks before the onset of his illness, and had allowed the puppy to sleep on the bed with him. Appropriate laboratory testing identified his illness as toxocariasis; treatment was instituted and his eye was saved.

Just how common is toxocariasis? No one knows for sure. It isn't a reportable disease, so, unlike measles or polio, no records of actual cases are kept. When I went to medical school, some sixty years ago, we were taught that man was immune to the worms of dogs. The first reported case of toxocariasis in man to appear in the medical literature was thirty-eight years ago.

When the American Veterinarian Medical Association met in Seattle in January 1979, a prominent veterinarian made this statement: "Toxocariasis infection in humans is more frequent and can have more serious consequences than was previously believed; in fact, toxocariasis may already be one of the more common parasitic infections in the United States." The *British Medical Journal* of September 1970 reported that the incidence of infection by the toxocaral larva is about 2 percent in adults in Britain. In this country, an occasional case is reported in the literature—there seems to be very little interest in the disease.

There are physicians, especially in Europe, who feel that there are wider implications from the toxocaral larva in man. The toxocaral larva is literally a "world traveler" in the human body: in its migration through blood vessels and lymph channels, it reaches all organs, and because of its size (0.02 mm), it causes physical damage that can open the door for other infections, such as pneumonia, hepatitis, and retinitis. There is even evidence that some cases of so called idiopathic epilepsy are actually due to toxocaral invasion of the brain.

How do you know if you have the disease? This will depend on which organ is invaded by the larvae. For example, if the lungs are involved, the symptoms will be much the same as if you had a viral or bacterial pneumonia.

How then is toxocariasis diagnosed? Most importantly, the

attending physician must be aware and suspicious of the disease. A clue may be found in an ordinary blood count and blood smear. Patients who have toxocariasis will usually be anemic and have an elevated white blood cell count. A great number of bright-pink-staining cells called eosinophils, up to 30 percent or more, will be found in the blood smear. Ordinarily, only about 1 percent of the white blood cells are eosinophils. Anemia, elevated white blood cell count, and an increase in eosinophils do not mean that the patient has toxocariasis. Other diseases and conditions can show the same findings, but when these three are found, toxocariasis is a real possibility, and should be ruled out by further testing.

The sure way to diagnose the disease is to demonstrate the larvae. They, however, are small, and because as few as twenty may cause significant illness or lesions, it's difficult to find them. In the eye, a single larva can cause a growth; I found two such cases reported in the literature. In large organs, like the liver and lungs, they are even harder to recover—the physician would have to remove several pieces of the suspected organ before finding the larvae. This is hazardous, and not many patients would allow it. But biopsies aren't necessary: a skin test, much like the tuberculin test, is available. Unfortunately, it's not 100 percent accurate. A blood test has been developed that appears to be very sensitive and specific for diagnosing toxocariasis: the Enzyme Linked Immunosorbent Assay, called ELISA, for short.

What can we do to control toxocariasis? We must get rid of the worms in dogs and cats. Rabies was controlled by forced immunization of all dogs and cats; this same law could be extended to include periodic worming of all dogs and cats. All dog owners should be educated to the necessity that they immediately remove the feces their dogs deposit in public places. Not only are these fouling up our lawns, beaches, and public places, but also, more importantly, they threaten our health. Our elected officials should be made aware of the reality that toxocariasis is widespread and is an important cause of morbidity—and that this needs attention.

Fortunately, the prognosis is good. Like a cold, the disease is usually self-limited, but as I have recorded, it can and sometimes does cause serious complications. All dogs and cats should be de-wormed under veterinary direction, and sand boxes that children play in should be covered when not in use.

I often wonder how many of us were told we had flu, or just a mild infection, when in fact we might have had toxocariasis.

Chapter 16

Sex Is Forever

Pour quoi Pas? Why Not?

Many years ago, I was painting the outside furniture at my mother-in-law's home in a retirement community. I had brought along my German shepherd and had tied him to the porch railing. Along came one of the elderly ladies who lived in the project. Steadying her walk with the help of a cane, she stopped and asked if the dog was friendly, and, if so, could she pet him. I answered that the dog was "like a baby" and loved to be petted.

"Like a baby, you say. Don't you know that we too love to be petted?" she responded with a visible smirk. "You have a lot to learn," she added. As she turned and walked away I heard her murmur, "And someone said you were a doctor—not mine, thank God!"

I was left perplexed. I really didn't understand how what I said could have disturbed her so much, but I dismissed it as a quirky remark from a senile woman. However, about four years later, her words popped into my mind; it was then that I first realized how right she'd been. Here's why and how:

In the town where I practiced, there lived a physician, not much older than I, who had a very large medical practice. This in itself wasn't unusual; what made him unique and set him apart from the other physicians in the community was his ability to draw and help men and women over fifty years of age. I treated older patients too, but his seemed to walk lighter and smile more, dressed better than mine, and were richer. They were the ones involved in civic activities, on the boards of corporations. They played golf and tennis, they were the joke tellers at parties and private clubs, and they had the energy and enthusiasm of youth. His patients, like mine, had their share of cancer, heart disease, and arthritis, etc., but somehow, they seemed to savor the pleasures and purpose of life in a way that my patients failed to do.

He prescribed the same medications that I did. He wasn't a "shot doctor. " In fact, he did nothing different than I, *except,* he always included a thorough sexual history on all his patients, old and young, and most importantly, he patiently took time to stress its importance and need.

At first, I dismissed him as some kind of "sex nut" who attracted a like sort, but as time passed and I had the opportunity to observe and reflect on his results, I realized how much more he offered his patients than I was able to.

It was then I decided to include a sexual history on all my patients when doing a complete physical examination. It wasn't easy for me to do. I don't recall ever hearing a lecture on sex while in medical school, or at a staff meeting after graduating. That arthritic old woman was right when she said, "You have a lot to learn."

I combed the literature and daily rehearsed what I would ask and say to my patients. I knew it had to be honest, sound, and meaningful. Never was I to embarrass, intimidate, or exploit the patient. A sexual history plays an important part in making a correct diagnosis.

I remember Ms. Adams, who came to my office every week with

a different complaint that I always failed to diagnose. Finally, I took a sexual history and discovered that her complaints and varied symptoms arose from the fact that she'd learned that her husband preferred homosexuality. It took only two office visits to convince her that only she was responsible for feeling sick every day; it was her decision alone. She could do nothing to change her husband. She must exercise her conscience and either live with him and her illnesses, or leave him. She chose to divorce, and soon moved to another state, so I don't know if she found happiness.

Ms. Barkley brought in her crying nine-year-old son and demanded that I tell him to stop masturbating, because it was evil and would make him sterile. It took several office visits to convince her that she was wrong, and to help the boy regain his self-esteem. I saw them separately and together. I never could tell her son that his mother was wrong. I tried to help him by suggesting that he engage in other activities such as sports, science, music, and the arts. Somehow, he would find something he could really like and be proud of. At an office visit, when his mother wasn't present, I devoted the entire fifteen-minute appointment to the subject of astronomy. I began, "Billy, the next time you get the urge to seek pleasure in your own body, don't. Get out of bed and look out your window and stare at the night sky, instead. You'll find it filled with stars. Think awhile, and ponder the mystery of it all. What are they made of? Why are they constantly exploding? Will they stay forever or disappear? Some are assembled into bodies we call constellations; we give them names like Scorpio, Leo, and Capricorn, and we give them names that we attach to the months of the year."

I then asked him, "When is your birthday?'

"April 21," he responded immediately.

"You are Taurus, the bull," I said. "How many stars make up your Taurus the bull? There are too many stars and they're too far away to count. Sailors use the constellations for direction when navigating the seas, just as street signs let us know where we are in a city. Besides constellations, if you look closely, you'll see huge clumps of stars smashed together. We call them galaxies. We really don't know why they are there, and for what reason they group together."

"Gosh! I didn't know that," he said with delight.

"Yes, and there's much more," I replied.

"More!" he exclaimed in disbelief.

"That's right. Recently, astronomers, people who spend their entire lifetimes studying the sky, discovered something so big and so far away that no one believes it could possibly exist. These bodies look like stars, but they're just too big to be stars, and they're even more mashed together than our galaxies. They give off the most powerful radio waves we've ever detected, but we can't understand a thing they are sending. We call these newly discovered objects "quasars." There's not a person on this earth today who has any idea what a quasar is. It's the farthest away, the largest, and the brightest object ever discovered in the sky above us. Study the sky; its mystery will fascinate you forever. You'll love it like nothing before. Never stop searching for things that can make you wiser and better."

Knock, knock...

"Yes."

"Doctor Parker, you're ten minutes late for your next appointment."

"I'm leaving now, but please talk to me again," said Billy as he was going.

"I will."

This boy remembered. Today he is an astronomer at a well-known university. I never again forgot what the little old lady in the retirement settlement told me: "Like a baby, you say. Don't you know that we too love to be petted? You have a lot to learn." I finally realized that she was simply telling me, "Without sex, none of us would be here now. Why dismiss it as short lived?"

When we are young, sex tends to be explosive, and primarily

a physical pleasure or a means to have children, but sex is much more than athletics and reproduction—it's the ability to become emotional and communicative. You must recognize and share your feelings in word and actions. It's an art to achieve mutual tenderness and kindness; it takes years of giving and receiving. The rewards bring bountiful possibilities for new emotional experience. You have to know what pleases your partner and what pleases you. You have to stop criticizing, and learn to laugh, tease, tell stories, and confess fears and uncertainties. Don't forget to cry and express passion. Sex after sixty can become even better than it was when you were young, and may last until you're in your nineties. If you're old and have no partner, don't hesitate to experience sex alone. It's your right, and it's not immoral—in fact, it's healthy, because it gives you a strong sense of self-esteem and worth.

If you have no interest in sex, that's OK. It's your prerogative. Abstention is nothing to feel guilty about: it won't make you ill, and it's not evil except if employed for spite or revenge. Coitus is sometimes impossible because of illness or structural defects. Remember, there's much more to sex than the physical union of male and female genitalia. Filling your life with kindness is what's most important. Enjoy each day as best you can. Breathe deeply the sweetness of the great outdoors and the splendor of each day, be it wet or dry. Never stop searching for things that can make you wiser and better. Life is not a farce—life is the greatest gift you'll ever receive.

Turn your eyes upward and ponder the enigma of the sky. You'll find a star dancing, and under that one you were born. Quien sabe?—Who knows what tomorrow will bring?

Chapter 17

Doctors Are No Damned Good

I try my best to avoid cocktail parties. Crowded, smoke-filled rooms bother my breathing and vision. The constant, uninhibited cacophonous chatter hurts my ears and leaves me with a headache. Each time I get home from such an affair, I swear I'll never go again, but...

Last week was no exception. The only difference at this party was that most of the conversation was directed toward doctors and the way they practice medicine. No one was talking about President Bush, Africa, or taxes. I walked about the room, Scotch in hand, looking for someone interesting to talk to about food, fishing, or sex—not necessarily in that order. Instead, all I could find were small groups of bodies huddled together, talking in earnest and totally oblivious to my presence. As I pushed my way past them, I couldn't help overhearing their remarks:

"Doctors are no damned good; all they want to do is treat disease, they're not interested in preventing illness."

"My doctor is so far behind the times, he actually laughed when I told him taking Vitamin E improved my sex life."

"Doctors are so blind to suffering, all they're interested in is money, money, money."

"Hey! You know I heard of a doctor who makes house calls. She lives in the Oregon hills and only charges three bucks for a call. Still uses her horse and buggy. Ain't many like that left."

"I went to a doctor last week because I have this cough that I'm sure is due to some deficiency in my body—you know, like zinc or manganese. Well, the old guy pounded my chest, listened to my breathing through some ancient hose, and then told me to stop smoking. Fifty dollars he charged me for that asinine advice."

"Doctors! Someone should tell those charlatans that it's about time they got out of their golf carts and began preventing illness instead of waiting for it to develop."

"Hell, they'll never tell you how to prevent disease. Why should they? There's a lot more money in treatment."

"My bypass operation cost me five thousand, and that doesn't include the assistant, the anesthetist, or the hospital bill. I've gone to my doctor regularly for over twenty years. Why didn't he give me something to prevent clogging in my heart vessels?"

"Where could you find an easier job than a doctor's? God cures ninety percent of our illnesses. The doctor bills us for all of them and we pay. Name me another profession where a silent partner does ninety percent of the work."

And so on, *ad infinitum.*

My glass was empty. It was a long hazardous haul back to the bar, so I stepped into the garden, hopped over a hedge, and got into my car and drove home, instead.

The quiet of my living room was a welcome relief, but was quickly overshadowed by self-reproach. I shouldn't have run out; I should have demonstrated some intestinal fortitude and answered those specious outbursts. Maybe I should go back, get up on the piano, and shout, "Listen you ingrates, you spurious intellectuals, stop your wailing and grumbling and hear me out. I've told many of you here, on more than one occasion, to stop killing yourselves, but apparently you either go deaf or develop a mental block in a doctor's office. Listening to you would make anyone believe that no doctor has ever heard of preventive medicine. Have you forgotten that Hippocrates, the father of medicine, advised temperance in food and drink as a means of preventing heart and brain disease? He lived 400 years before Christ. Today doctors still preach the same truths.

"I would like to go on record and say to you, loud and clear, that to practice preventive medicine one must also alter lifestyles that bring on disease, and that means ordering people around. I'm against doctors becoming law officers or dictators.

My job, like any other doctor's, is to instruct and advise, and that I have done. But if you want me to lay down the law, I'll start right here and now.

"Jim! I've told you time and again to stop smoking. As of now, I forbid you to kill yourself with lung cancer. Give me your cigarettes!

"Mary, hand me your drink. I told you Tuesday that your serum bilirubin was elevated. Now, damn it, you're not going to die of cirrhosis of the liver. You are not to take another drop of liquor in any form!

"You, Phil, what the hell are you snickering about? That hole you have in your nasal septum isn't going to get any smaller. In fact, if you don't get to the plastic surgeon your nose is going to collapse. I told you a long time ago that if you continued to sniff cocaine this would happen.

"Hey, George! I've seen you go to the bathroom five times in the past hour. If you've got the clap again, as I suspect, you can be sure I'll tell your wife the truth this time. I've had it making excuses for you.

"Marge, why don't you tell the people here why you come to my office every Monday morning with a so-called migraine? You and I know it's because you're shacking up with Fred while your husband is out playing golf on the weekends. No more tranquilizers for you. Either you give up Fred, or suffer the headaches—I'm not going to contribute to your becoming a drug addict.

"Dave, tomorrow you'll give notice at work that you're quitting. I'm not going to wait for you to develop an ulcer. You've already admitted to me that your pain is entirely due to your nerve-racking work.

"Get away from the shrimp, Joanne. You know they're loaded with cholesterol. Remember the drawing I showed you at the office, of how cholesterol and fat form plaques in the walls of the arteries? And have you forgotten your last treadmill test? Well, I'll tell you again: that S T segment depression means your coronary arteries already have significant plaque formation, so it's back on your diet or I schedule you for bypass surgery.

"Hazel, hand me your car keys. You're too drunk to drive. If you don't give a damn for your own life, have some consideration for the poor people in the other cars."

I could re-inform all of them about the dangers of overindulging in food, drink, play, and work, but who listens? Besides, I'm tired and had better get to bed.

THREE A.M.

Brrring! Brrring! Brrring!

"Hello."

"Doctor Parker?"

"Yes."

"This is Memorial Hospital. Doctor Jack Gannon in emergency wants to talk to you. May I connect you?"

"Yes, please. Thank you."

"Hello."

"Hello, Doctor Parker?"

"Yes."

"This is Jack in emergency."

"Yes, Jack, what's up?"

"I have a Hazel Donnelly here; says she's a patient of yours."

"Yes, she is."

"Well, the paramedics brought her in about thirty minutes ago. She has second- and third-degree burns over fifty percent of her body. Luckily, her face is spared. She admits to smoking in bed—guess they'll never learn. I did a cut-down on her and have a bottle of Ringer's running. Blood has already been sent to the lab for typing, chemistry, and gases. I sedated her and she's now fairly comfortable. Is there anything else you want me to do?"

"No, thanks, Jack. You did well. Tell Hazel I'll be there in a few minutes."

I failed to practice preventive medicine. Forgive me, *mea culpa.*

Chapter 18

A Little Boy

"Doctor, why did you wash your hands before and after you examined me? My mother made me take a bath before I came here; why didn't you?"

The mother grasped his shoulder and shook him with disgust. "Don't ever say such a bad thing again," she blurted.

I was taken by surprise, paused, and then said to the boy, "Billy, that's a very good question." I then told him briefly about germs on the hands and how the bad ones can spread disease.

"Oh, thanks," he answered, "Now I know why you washed your hands." I said nothing to the mother regarding the incident. That evening, while relaxing in my den, I thought about this boy and why I hadn't talked to his mother alone. I should have explained to her that his question demonstrated a very thoughtful and inquisitive mind, and that she should encourage his asking "Why?" and never condemn him for doing so.

That five-year-old was no blockhead. His question demonstrated a very organized mind. He wanted to know why and wasn't afraid to ask. He vividly demonstrated what the great Greek philosopher, Socrates, taught his students to do, long before Christ was born. I should have sat down with his mother and talked about Socrates, who was born in Athens and became the leading philosopher of Greece. He was a brilliant teacher who was interested only in thinking and talking about humanity's problems. His guiding rule was "Know thyself." He believed that goodness was based on wisdom, and wickedness on ignorance. No wise person would deliberately choose what was bad for him in the long run, but most people, through ignorance, might choose an evil that appeared to be good at the time.

To gain wisdom you must search for it. When your parents, friends, or elders tell you something, or you see something you don't understand, you must ask "Why?" For this teaching, Socrates was charged with corrupting the youth of Athens. At trial he was found guilty and condemned to death. Even in his last days in prison, he instructed his visitors, friends, and jailers to take nothing for granted, and to ask "Why?" in pursuit of wisdom. According to his greatest pupil, Plato, Socrates spent his last day discussing the immortality of the soul. At sunset, the jailer brought him the cup of hemlock. The great philosopher raised it to his lips, made a toast to the gods, and drank the bitter poison. He met death as he had lived, with calm and self-control.

Many is the time I've wondered what my patient, "Billy, the kid" did with his life.

Chapter 19

Question #1

Question:

How come doctors put patients on restrictive diets and in turn frequent the best restaurants?

—Mrs. Xavier

Answer:

Good question. I can't speak for all physicians, but I'll be happy to tell you what I do. We all must eat; if we ate nothing, our lives would end in just a few days. Some of you are restricted because you're allergic to certain foods; you have a condition or illness that is worsened if you eat fats, excess sugar, or salt, or if you're just plain overweight. Most people eat only to appease their hunger, or because it's breakfast, lunch, or dinnertime. So do I, but two or three times a month I splurge, and pick a fine restaurant that caters to my appetite and emotion. It's absolutely independent of hunger; the food is created with artful skill and made with good fresh ingredients, and hopefully accompanied by true friends and enough time to savor.

There's nothing more appealing to me than veal cooked in Marsala wine by an Italian chef. Most good chefs, and especially the French, won't use water for cooking when they can use wine. Wine and spirits lose their alcohol in cooking, but the essential flavor remains.

Once the food is placed before me, the only spice I use is fresh-ground pepper. It doesn't make foot "hot"—its real function is to strengthen and emphasize the natural flavor of the food.

Ask your doctor if you can splurge, and, if so, how often. You might not get the answer you hope for, but at least you've tried.

Chapter 20

Black Pepper, King of Spices

When I was medical director at Rockwell International Space Division, I had a staff physician who literally drove me nuts watching him eat. No matter what we had, he covered it all with black pepper before taking a bite. One day I called him to come to my office and I asked him why. His answer was brief and to the point: "You know I was born in Persia. We had no refrigeration and very little money. My mother often had to serve us tainted food. She would tell us children to sprinkle it with pepper and it would taste good. We did, and I still do, just from habit and because it tastes much better."

I thanked the Persian doctor and told him to keep it up.

That brief conversation made me very curious, so I visited a local library and combed several encyclopedias to find out all I could about pepper. I discovered that, contrary to common belief, pepper doesn't make food "hot." Its real function is to increase the appetite, whip up the intestines to increase their juices, and make tainted food edible. Pepper doesn't have a strong aroma.

No one knows for sure when or where pepper was first found. It was probably on the southwest coast of India, because the world still gets most of its pepper from this area today. Through stealth it found its way into Sumatra, an Indonesian island that is now is the world's second largest pepper producer.

History tells us that, thousands of years ago, Arabs carried pepper on camelback from western India, through the areas now called Pakistan, Afghanistan, Iran, Iraq, and Syria, to the coast of the Mediterranean Sea. It was a treacherous trip hampered by thieves and pirates, and took more than two years to complete. This pepper trade was a monopoly of the Arabs, who each year raised the price of pepper. The Romans got angry and went to war against the Arabs. Their intent was to conquer the Arab kingdoms, but they lost. However, the Arab victory didn't last long because of a Greek merchant who lived during the reign of the Roman Emperor Claudius (A.D. 41–54). The Greek's place of business was in southeast Egypt, on the shore of the Red Sea. He discovered that he could get to India by sailing down the Red Sea and then across the Arabian Sea. It no longer was necessary to trespass on lands controlled by Arabs, and he could do it in less than a year. That put an end to the Arab monopoly—the price of pepper dropped significantly.

Canning and refrigeration were still unknown, but now most Mediterraneans and Europeans could afford to sprinkle their tainted food and make it edible. In addition, they soon learned that the taste and odor of fresh food could be strengthened. Gourmet cooking took a great leap forward and the master chef was born—it was a time to rejoice.

In A.D. 408, one of the Germanic kings prized pepper so highly that when he conquered Rome he demanded and received as tribute 3,000 pounds of pepper. Five hundred years later, King Ethelred II of England loved his pepper so much that he imposed a tax of ten pounds of pepper on all foreign imports.

In 1295, Marco Polo and his two brothers returned to Venice. They had traveled by caravan across Asia into China. In China (Cathay, as it was then called), the Polos had become friends of Kublai Khan, grandson of Genghis Khan, the Mongol conqueror of central Asia. Marco Polo mentioned the immense profits Kublai Khan had obtained from the pepper trade, emphasizing that ten thousand pounds of pepper were handled through the seaport of Hangchow every day; the merchants of Europe found that hard to believe.

It took another 200 years before Vasco da Gama, a Portuguese navigator, discovered the first all-sea route to India via the Cape of Good Hope at the southern tip of Africa. At about the same time, an Italian, Christopher Columbus, was convincing King Ferdinand and Queen Isabella of Spain that he could reach India much faster by sailing west instead of east. They gambled and gave him three ships and eighty-seven sailors. He landed in what is now called North America, but thought he was in India. On the island of Jamaica he discovered a berry that he called pepper. When he arrived in Spain he found out it wasn't pepper, but allspice, a potpourri of the aromas of cloves, cinnamon, nutmeg, and mace, but he did find the orchid whose seedpods produce vanilla.

After Vasco da Gama accomplished the all-sea route to India, Portugal lost no time in colonizing Goa on the west coast of India. From there they monopolized the pepper and spice trade until 1599. Then, in came the Dutch to conquer the Portuguese colony, which they held on to for almost 200 years.

By this time England had tired of watching Holland get rich selling pepper, so they went to war with Holland, dislodging the Dutch from all the Asian spice lands except for Java in Indonesia. Controlling the sale of pepper, England reaped profits beyond her wildest expectations. During this time a Boston-born young man named Elihu Yale worked as a clerk for the British East India Company. Yale later became governor of Madras in India, and made a fortune in pepper, which he later used to found Yale University.

The United States got into the pepper-trading act at the time England monopolized the source. American ships sailed into India, and bargained the British East India Company to the lowest price. They then loaded their ships with pepper and sailed back to Salem, Massachusetts where they sold it at a 700 percent profit. This lasted for twenty years, until piracy and greed put an end to the perverse doings.

During World War II, the Japanese took control of the waters off India and Indonesia. The American housewife had to make do with a pepper that was 95 percent ground cereals and only 5 percent real pepper. Ironically, most people didn't know the difference.

Black pepper is the fruit of a plant called *Piper nigrum,* a vine that can grow thirty feet tall. Each vine is covered with shiny black leaves. Twice each year, every vine will send out new growths, which are long, thin spikes—up to twenty on each vine. On each one of these spikes some fifty or more white flowers will bloom, then develop into pepper berries. The spikes are harvested when the green berries are just beginning to turn red. Otherwise, allowed to ripen fully, the pepper won't be at its best and most pungent. The spikes are then spread on mats to dry in the sun. The whole dry berries are sold in the markets as peppercorns, and used by gourmets to spice and dress meats.

The ordinary black pepper bought in the market is simply the dried, shriveled black pepper berry that has been ground. Allowing these same berries to ripen fully on the vine to a dark red produces white pepper: the berries are picked and soaked in water so that they can be peeled by hand or by machine. After they are dried, they are sold whole as white peppercorns, or are ground and sold as white pepper.

I cannot distinguish the difference between white and black pepper. The French gourmet, however, will tell you the flavor of the white pepper is much milder and more delicate—and it doesn't make ugly black spots on light-colored foods.

The Italian gourmet will use only black pepper that comes from the northern part of the Malabar district of India, and it has to be grown and harvested after the first monsoon in January, not the second, and lighter, April monsoon. He will emphasize that the heavier downpour of the first monsoon gives the pepper its full body, strong aroma, and delectable flavor. Besides, it looks so good in salami and sausage.

Black pepper has been used, without benefit, for centuries, to treat intestinal, urinary, and sexual problems.

Over fifty years ago, when I first started to deliver babies, I remember reading in a very proper obstetrical textbook a glowing report on how to treat difficult and prolonged labor by the "Quill method." One would take a quill (chicken feather) and fill it will freshly ground black pepper, hold it firmly, pass it under the nostrils of the laboring woman, and have her inhale it deeply. This would bring on violent sneezing, which profoundly increased abdominal pressure and blew the baby out.

Of course, we're gentler and kinder today, and certainly more learned. We teach our patients to relax and accept the pain. But when the labor gets tough and prolonged, the father, acting as quarterback, takes over. He has been programmed to remind his wife over and over to relax between contractions and then to hold her breath, close her mouth, and push, push, *push* when the pain recurs. If that doesn't work, usually after an hour or two, she is mercifully wheeled to surgery, where she is anesthetized, her lower abdomen split, and the baby removed. If you think the quill treatment was cruel, just try to imagine what obstetricians in the year 2050 will think of our treatment today for difficult and prolonged labor.

I really hope you will continue to enjoy your pepper, be it black or white, even though it costs over eight dollars a pound. You can live without it—but why should you? Hail to the king!

Chapter 21

Childbirth Fever

As a child, I surreptitiously overheard my grandmother warn my mother not to have her baby in the hospital.

"Why?" my mother asked.

"Because you might *die* in the hospital," Grandma expressed emphatically. The word "die" frightened me. I remember running into the backyard, hiding behind a big bush, and crying. I didn't want my mother to die. "Please, God, don't let her die," I repeated over and over.

A few days later, my mother delivered a healthy girl at home with only my grandmother's help. I soon forgot about my crying jag. It wasn't until I was in high school that, one day, a hygiene teacher lectured about a "fever" that killed a lot of women when they chose childbirth in a hospital, instead of delivering at home with the aid of a midwife, relative, or friend. This awakened my memory of Grandma's warning. The teacher quoted unbelievable but true statistics: between the years 1600 and 1850, one half of the women having their babies in the best Paris hospitals died; in Berlin, one out of three, and in Edinburgh nearly one hundred percent died. She called it "puerperal fever," puerperal meaning occurring during childbirth or in the period immediately following.

Why did these women die? The answer was before their eyes, but it took more than 250 years to discover. Physicians knew nothing of antisepsis; bacteria hadn't yet been discovered. Medical students learned obstetrics studying the cadavers of women who, in most cases, had died of puerperal fever. Physicians would teach these students by handling the diseased organs and demonstrating the pathology in detail. If your clothes and hands got stained with blood, it showed you were really paying attention and learning a lot. From the autopsy room the student and physician would go directly to the obstetrical ward to examine or deliver the patient, with their instruments and hands unwashed.

Puerperal sepsis was known in antiquity, but it was a rare complication of childbirth. Then, physicians didn't deliver babies, and hospitals, which were few, strongly discouraged women from coming to the hospital for childbirth. Almost all babies born before 1600 were delivered at home with the aid of a midwife or friend. The only time a physician was called was when there was a serious complication, such as uncontrollable hemorrhage or failed labor (inability to deliver the baby). Most patients would die from complications brought on by the physician. He labored under useless or ignorant procedures, such as bloodletting, hot compresses, non-sterile instruments, or ineffective medications. In China, many women delivered themselves in rice fields with no help and seldom a complication. Can you imagine a deadly epidemic lasting over 250 years? Only the Lord knows how many mothers died needlessly. How slowly we learn.

In 1818 a child was born in Budapest, the capital of Hungary. The fourth of eight children of an obscure family of small merchants, he was named Ignaz Semmelweis. He never learned to spell or punctuate; he deplored grammar, which kept him from publishing his momentous discovery until shortly before he died. To please his father, who wanted him to be a lawyer, he entered the University of Pest, then after two years transferred to the University of Vienna to study law. He hated the subject, and spent most of his time carousing in student "coffee houses." There he met a friend who was a medical student at the same university. One day his friend invited him to watch an autopsy. He was so stimulated by the dissection that, with his parents' permission, he transferred immediately to the Vienna Medical School. A preeminent student, he never missed a class, and spent many extra hours experimenting and practicing dissection in the autopsy room.

Ignaz Semmelweis received his medical degree in 1844, and then decided to specialize in obstetrics and gynecology. At that time it required only six months to be certified a specialist. Several professors recognized his ability and incessant enthusiasm for work in the delivery room, surgery, and autopsy room. He was soon appointed first assistant to Dr. Johann Klein, chief of the Lying-in Hospital in Vienna. Klein respected Semmelweis' industriousness, but showed little interest in his autopsy work.

Semmelweis was overwhelmed examining patients, operating, supervising difficult deliveries, and teaching, but he never gave up doing autopsies, though it meant getting up at dawn to go to the morgue and perform his work on a puerperal fever victim before making rounds with his students on the obstetrical ward. He noted in dismay that, despite the special attention he gave his patients, his first month as first assistant to Chief Dr. Klein was seriously marred by the fact that more patients died of puerperal fever than ever had before in a single month. He found that in the

First Obstetrical Clinic where he and Dr. Klein worked, mortality was much higher than in the adjoining clinic. The First Clinic was for the rich, the Second Clinic for the poor.

After painstaking comparisons, Ignaz tabulated the mortality in the two clinics. In the previous year, the First Clinic had three times the number of deaths from puerperal fever than the Second Clinic, even though the Second Clinic had many more patients. He recited his findings to his chief; Dr. Klein listened, but took it as a direct criticism of his work, so he demoted Semmelweis, who returned to his room heartbroken and cried himself to sleep. The very next day he read how Dr. Robert Collins, chief of the famous Rotunda Hospital in Dublin, controlled a puerperal fever epidemic by fumigating the hospital with chlorine gas. Semmelweis at once began to study English in hopes of transferring to Dublin; he never got there. He approached Dr. Klein and asked if he could have the Lying-in Hospital sprayed with chlorine to rid it of puerperal fever. The chief, without hesitation, responded, "Absolutely not—the article you read makes no sense."

Each day Ignaz became more agitated. No one would take his recommendation seriously. His performance in the delivery and surgery rooms was noticeably deteriorating. Dr. Josef Skoda, professor of Internal Medicine at the hospital, made Ignaz take a month's vacation, which he spent at a resort in Venice. Enjoying himself, he relaxed completely, but his return to the Vienna hospital was marred by the news that one of his closest friends, Kolletschka, had died. Kolletschka had sustained a scalpel wound while performing an autopsy on a puerperal fever victim. Ignaz rushed at once to the pathology office, where he was overwhelmed when he read the report of the postmortem examination: the findings were identical with those in puerperal fever. The finger Kolletschka cut was abscessed, and the infection had spread to his lungs and abdomen—no organ was spared. Ignaz recognized immediately that Kolletschka had died in exactly the same way that the puerperal fever patients in the obstetrical ward had.

He later wrote, "God only knows the number of women whom I consigned prematurely to the grave, for I occupied myself with the cadavers to a degree reached by few obstetricians."

Without consultation, Ignaz wasted no time: he ordered all on duty at the hospital to wash their hands in chlorinated water after every examination. Also, everything that came in contact with the patient had to be washed—clothing, bed sheets, bedpans, and instruments. Physicians, students, and aides all objected to being treated like children. However, Semmelweis maintained his stand, and spoke out at every lecture he gave: it was the doctors themselves who spread the disease by not cleaning their hands. They and the medical students carried the "sepsis" from the morgue to the clinic. Opponents of his idea ridiculed and attacked him fiercely. Even Dr. Klein harassed Semmelweis, because the laundry bills grew too high, but he could do little more, because, for the first time in the history of this great hospital, there were no deaths in the First Clinic for a year.

In 1850 Hungary experienced a short revolt for independence. Semmelweis was one of the first to join the Hungarian rebels fighting for liberty. They put up a good fight, but were routed by the combined Austrian and Russian Armies. Ignaz wasn't wounded and returned to the Lying-in Hospital in Vienna. Dr. Klein, a royalist, promptly fired him for participating in the revolt.

Ignaz returned to Budapest where he got a hero's welcome, because the people considered it patriotic that a former first assistant at such a famous Vienna hospital would return to a country where medicine was in such a lamentable state. He soon developed a large practice in obstetrics and gynecology and became head of the OB-GYN division of St. Rockus Hospital in Pest. Forthwith, he established chlorine washing, over the bitter opposition of the staff, long accustomed to slovenly habits. By the end of a year, for the first time in the history of any European hospital except Vienna in 1847, deaths from puerperal fever were less than 1 percent.

That didn't stop the criticism Semmelweis got from all of Europe. He continued to work and teach in Pest, but he began to scream at his medical students who failed to wash their hands. Articles he read in medical magazines from Paris and Berlin added to his agitation, because they either never mentioned his work or remarked that it was worthless. Finally, in 1857, he got so enraged that he wrote his first book, *Etiology, Concept and Prophylaxis of Puerperal Fever.* It didn't sell, and some physicians called it "humbug."

In the same year Ignaz, then thirty-eight, met and married a beautiful girl of eighteen. She was the perfect spouse for a temperamental genius. They had five children, two of whom died in infancy.

By 1865, Semmelweis' usual tendency to moodiness increased. He hardly spoke to his colleagues; then his lectures became unintelligible to his students. He yelled at them for no apparent reason. His friends and family forced him to a sanatorium in Vienna. The examining physician discovered an infected wound on the middle finger of the right hand. He told the family that Ignaz was very ill and had to be taken to a general hospital.

Just ten days earlier, Semmelweis had performed an autopsy on a victim of puerperal fever. He was so intent that he never noticed nicking his finger. He had struggled all his life against ignorance and prejudice to save the lives of mothers. On a summer morning in 1865, he died of puerperal fever. He was forty-seven years old.

It wasn't until 1879, fourteen years later, that the Frenchman Louis Pasteur, one of the outstanding bacteriologists of all time, isolated the *streptococcus* bacteria from a puerperal fever patient. During a tumultuous meeting of the French Academy, he thundered, "It is not miasma nor anything else but the nursing and medical staffs who carry this bacteria from an infected woman to a healthy one."

Yes, it was the doctors that killed the patients, not, as they claimed, a poisonous atmosphere rising from a swamp. My grandma was right when she said to my mother, "Don't go to the hospital—you might die."

Chapter 22

Right Or Wrong?

It was a beautiful day, the sky dressed in puffy white clouds scattered in brilliant blue. The warm air was perfumed with the scent of the orange trees in full bloom across the street from my office. I sat relaxed in the consulting room. Lazily, I rubbed my eyes and mused: God! Those were good-looking twins I delivered at six a.m. I thought the father would go through the roof when I told him he had two healthy boys. How can you describe such joy? And how can you paint the relief I saw in Mr. Nielsen's face when I told him the tumorous uterus I had just removed from his wife was not malignant and she would soon be home again? This is the full life, and I wouldn't trade it with anyone.

Knock—knock.

"Doctor, are you ready? Your patient is all set and waiting for you in Room 1. Here's her chart; her blood pressure and urine are normal."

"Good morning, Mrs. Waters. How are you this gorgeous day?"

"I'm all right, but my feet are beginning to swell, especially in the evening."

In the far corner of the room, her four-year-old son was trying to open a cabinet drawer.

"Please don't touch those drawers," I said. "Now, Mrs. Waters, let's see, your blood pressure is normal and the urine is normal." As she lay on the examining table, I proceeded with the routine exam. "The baby's heart tones are clear and regular at 140 beats per minute. That's fine. The swelling in your feet today is minimal. Your baby is due in five weeks and your uterus measures thirty-five centimeters, so we're right on target. Swelling of the feet is common and you needn't be concerned by it. Jimmy, please don't touch those shelves, there are things in there that you can't play with."

"The swelling in my feet is only in the evening, I've told you."

"Yes, and if you'll raise them on a stool or the seat of a chair when you're resting in the evening, the swelling will go away. It's nothing serious. Stop, Jimmy—do not open those drawers."

His mother never said anything to her son. "Doctor, he's been complaining about a sore throat and won't eat. Would you look in his throat and see if he's getting strep throat?"

"Jimmy, come sit down on this stool and I'll look at your throat."

"*No,* I don't want to."

"Jimmy, sit down, like the doctor told you." Reluctantly, Jimmy did, but kept his head down, his chin on his chest.

"Jim! Bring your head up and open you mouth so I can see." He did—and suddenly spit in my face. His mother sat still and did nothing. I swung my hand and slapped him in the face, fairly hard. He cried aloud and grabbed his mother. She took him by the hand and started out the door, shouting, "I'll never come to this office again. You had no right to beat my son. You're a terrible doctor." She raved over and over as she rushed through the waiting room, full of patients, and left, slamming the front door. I never heard from her again.

That was over fifty years ago. I often wondered why I reacted so.

On Friday, May 18, 2001, I read in *The Los Angeles Times* that former President Clinton was hit by an egg while visiting Warsaw during a speaking tour. He laughed and said, "It's good for young people to be angry about something." On the same page I read that John Prescott, the number-two figure in

Britain's government, was splattered on the head with an egg at point-blank range. He lashed out instantly with a powerful left to the egg-thrower's jaw.

Was Clinton right or wrong?

Was Prescott right or wrong?

Was I right or wrong?

Chapter 23

Question #2

Question:

Six weeks ago, my best friend gave birth to a seven-pound, three-ounce baby. He looks normal but he whined real loud and jerked his body so bad that they had to keep him in the hospital. He wouldn't eat, so they fed him through tubes and needles for two weeks. He is home now, and still cries a lot but doesn't jerk as much. Her husband blames his wife and says she must have bad genes. She has told me that there has never been a bad child born on either side of her family. She also said that her husband sniffs cocaine and is always high on coke when they have sex. She has never used drugs, alcohol, or tobacco. Could her husband be the guilty one?

– Please don't print my name or address.

Answer:

If what you tell me is true, the father of this child is most likely to be the "guilty one". A group of physicians headed by Ricardo A. Yazigi, M.D. recently completed an extensive study at Washington University School of Medicine, in St. Louis, Missouri. This experiment proved conclusively that cocaine binds itself to sperm without injuring the sperm. By this process, the sperm can transport cocaine into an ovum (egg) and be the culprit in the abnormal development of the child. This study was published in the October 9, 1991 issue of the *Journal of the American Medical Association*—any doctor can show you the proof.

More and more evidence is emerging that not only cocaine, but also other drugs, can attach themselves to sperm without killing it or affecting its mobility. Alcohol and tobacco are suspected of damaging sperm, and it's highly possible that the damaged sperm can fertilize an egg and produce an unhealthy baby.

Some states are now prosecuting women who used drugs during pregnancy. It's time the lawyers took a look at the fathers and investigate whether or not they were on drugs at the time of conception.

Chapter 24

Birth-control Pills

Question:

My doctor won't renew my prescription for birth-control pills. He delivered our two children and I've always gone to him for my yearly physical examinations. When I asked what was wrong with me, he answered, "Absolutely nothing; you're healthy, but the pill is no longer safe for you because you're thirty-five years old. Use foam and condoms instead, but if you'd rather, I can tie your tubes or refer your husband for a vasectomy."

Neither my husband nor I want our tubes tied. I want to know why birth-control pills aren't safe after thirty-five. Can you help?

– J. I. Sacramento, Calif.

Answer:

Your doctor is not alone in giving this advice; in fact he may be in the majority. The reason for it is that in 1980 the Food and Drug Administration (FDA) required all drug companies to warn doctors and patients of the increased danger of heart attacks if the pill were taken after age thirty-five. The FDA based this warning on sound studies that were begun in 1968 and ended in 1979. At that time the pill was much more potent than what we use today; more importantly, the association between smoking and oral contraceptive use wasn't known. In other words, it was the smoking, and not the pill, that increased the risk of heart attack after thirty-five.

Two years ago, A.C.O.G., an organization made up exclusively of specialists in the field of obstetrics and gynecology, went on record saying, "Healthy nonsmoking women aged thirty-five to forty-four can continue to take oral contraceptives without fear of compromising their health."

Just a few months ago the FDA changed its mind and advised the producers of birth-control pills that they should modify their labeling to read, "The benefits of the use of oral contraception by healthy nonsmoking women forty or older may outweigh the possible risks."

Except for death, nothing in life is 100 percent certain. We all take risks: when we get out of bed, we risk breaking a leg; driving to work can kill us; even breathing Los Angeles air has its perils. We're constantly bombarded by risks from diverse sources. It's time we looked at the benefits.

Benefits you can derive from using birth-control pills:

1. *They safely and effectively prevent pregnancy.*
2. *You experience less menstrual bleeding and fewer cramps.*
3. *Salpingitis and ectopic pregnancy are less common.*
4. *Birth-control pills may slow down the process of osteoporosis.*
5. *Their use decreases the incidence of:*
   a. *Endometrial cancer;*
   b. *Uterine fibroids;*
   c. *Benign breast disease;*
   d. *Functional ovarian cysts;*
   e. *Ovarian cancer;*

f. And, it has been shown that protection against ovarian and endometrial cancer persists even after women stop using birth-control pills.

Your doctor sounds like a caring and conservative person. Call him; he might have a change of heart. If not, get a second opinion.

Chapter 25

Tales of Obstetrics

Labor is a natural process, you say, so why make such a big deal of it? Because complications can and do occur, often when you least expect them.

One evening I saw Marion in labor with a breech presentation. Marion was a nurse, and well versed in obstetrical complications. I had told her several weeks before that hers was a breech presentation, and reassured her that, since I had delivered her before, I knew her pelvic structure was such that a breech delivery posed no foreseeable problems.

A breech delivery is a situation where the baby is born butt first, instead of in the usual headfirst manner. A baby's butt is of lesser diameter than its head. Because of this, in a breech presentation there's more room for the cord to slip between the baby's butt and the mother's hipbones, and sometimes it does just that. This complication usually happens during labor as the baby, with each contraction of the uterus, slowly finds its way through the birth canal. It's especially more apt to happen when the fluid-filled sac in which the baby lives accidentally ruptures. The sudden gush of amniotic fluid washes the cord down with it, and the cord gets trapped between the baby's body and the mother's pelvis. Suddenly the flow of blood to the unborn child is cut off, leaving precious few minutes to save the child, whose life-sustaining air supply has been eliminated. It's no different than my grabbing you by the neck and choking you—unless I stopped, you'd soon die.

Everything was proceeding normally with Marion; her contractions were regular and she was about halfway through her labor, that is, the cervix or mouth of the womb was 50 percent dilated. The baby's heartbeat was steady; the monitor showed the normal 140 beats per minute. The baby's butt was making a steady descent through the birth canal. Marion was having an easy time with her third delivery, and even found time to chat with the attending nurse, with whom she had worked. I was down the hall in the doctors' lounge, my feet up on a footrest, watching Johnny Carson on the tube. Suddenly, the nurse shouted on the intercom, "Come quickly, Doctor Parker—the bag just ruptured and I can see the cord between Marion's legs."

I ran to Marion's room, slipped on a sterile glove, inserted my hand into the vagina and gently pushed the baby's butt upward in the birth canal, relieving the pressure on the cord. The monitor showed the baby's heart began to beat normally again. I soon discovered that there was no way to deliver the child safely from below, because Marion's cervix was still only half dilated—a Caesarean section was mandatory to save her baby's life.

Jim, another obstetrician, was dozing on a cot in the doctors' lounge, waiting for his patient to complete her labor. I had a nurse call him on the intercom. He came immediately, scrubbed his hands and put on sterile gloves, and his hand replaced mine in Marion's vagina. It was his job now to keep the baby's butt from compressing the cord with each of Marion's contractions, which were now coming harder and faster. In the meantime, the obstetrical nurse had already called the operating suite and made the arrangements for a Caesarean section. The nurse and I lifted Marion off the labor bed onto a cart, and quickly wheeled her down the long corridor to the operating room. Poor Jim—all 250 pounds of him—was doing his best to keep up with us, stooped over, while making sure his hand kept the baby's butt from constricting the cord.

In the operating room, Bill, the anesthesiologist, was awaiting our arrival. All but Jim helped transfer Marion from the cart to the operating table. We first turned her on her side so Bill could administer a spinal anesthetic. That soon relieved Marion's labor pains, and the baby stopped forcing its way down the birth canal. Jim, however, had to remain at his station, lifting the baby's butt so that the cord wasn't squashed.

I had finished scrubbing my hands, and was gowned and masked. After a sterile preparation of Marion's abdomen by the nurse, I stepped to the operating table. The surgical nurse handed me the knife. With one sweep, I carefully and easily went through all four layers of the abdomen: the skin, fat, fascia, and peritoneum. I then entered the exposed uterus by cutting through its musculature, and removed the baby—headfirst. The entire procedure took just minutes. I handed the baby boy to a surgical nurse who immediately held him head down. Using a small rubber bulb, she removed the mucus from his throat. He cried immediately and vigorously. I clamped and cut the umbilical cord, and the nurse handed the newborn to Marion, who couldn't have been happier.

Jim was now standing up straight again. With his aching back and numb hand, he scrubbed, gowned, and masked to assist me in the closure of the uterus and the abdominal wall. The closure took much more time than the delivery, as we had to make sure that all the bleeding points were eliminated and all tissue layers brought back to their original positions. Marion and her baby boy went home on the fifth day, happy and well.

On another occasion, I had just completed delivering a healthy baby for a young couple. The new mother was admiring and handling her child as it lay on her abdomen; Daddy stood beside her, his smile ear to ear. After the cord had stopped pulsating, I clamped, cut, and tied it, allowing the mother to put her newborn to her breast as she desired.

I waited twenty minutes for the afterbirth to separate and expel, but nothing happened. As was the custom, I rescrubbed, and put on a clean gown and sterile gloves. I then inserted my hand into the uterus to determine why the afterbirth wouldn't deliver. Exploring, I discovered that it was still firmly attached and wouldn't separate by the usual kneading and massaging of the uterus, so I proceeded to do a manual separation of the placenta. With my fingers, I tried to peel the afterbirth off the uterine wall, but found that it wouldn't peel. I was dealing with a condition called placenta acreata—the afterbirth had actually grown into the muscular wall of the uterus. There was no easy way to remove it safely; brisk bleeding soon followed, and I had to rush to surgery to remove the uterus, or the mother would have bled to death. Daddy fainted and a nurse had to revive him.

Fortunately, all went well. The mother and her husband made speedy recoveries and took home with them a lovely daughter. Of course, the mother will never again have a child of her own, because she no longer has a uterus.

One morning I was delivering a physician's wife of her eighth child. She had a very short but tumultuous labor; her husband, Jack, hardly had time to get her to the hospital. On arrival, she was taken immediately to the delivery room where I was waiting. Jack had called me at home before heading for the hospital.

After quick preparation of the perineal area, the child was born about three contractions later with absolutely no difficulty—no drugs, no anesthetic, no instruments were needed. While I was caring for the baby, the mother began to complain of feeling weak and dizzy. I wasted no time, only changed gloves and put my hand into her uterus. I found a hole in the wall large enough to allow my four fingers through it; she had obviously ruptured her uterus during labor and was bleeding internally. We had her on the operating table in minutes and removed her torn and bleeding uterus.

Poor Jack was badly shaken, never dreaming that he would be assisting at his wife's hysterectomy, but time was of the essence; I couldn't wait for another surgeon to arrive. Jack's wife had an uneventful recovery and six days later went home with a healthy baby boy.

I've given you three examples of serious complications that occur rarely but are far from unique. Other complications happen with much greater frequency, the most important and serious being unexplained hemorrhage right after delivery. The bleeding must be stopped and the blood volume replaced or the mother may lose her life. There's no way to predict which woman will bleed, rupture her uterus, prolapse a cord, or develop placenta acreta. There's no ultrasound, X-ray, or lab test that can forecast these occurrences. Like earthquakes, they happen without warning.

People, including some doctors, who profess that women can be screened beforehand, and that only those without complications should be allowed to deliver at home, are simply ignorant of the facts. I'm fully aware that most deliveries occur without complications and require no assistance. If you want statistics, call the health department; they'll refer you to the so-called authority. To me, statistics don't mean much. If a complication happens to you, then the rate of complications for you is still 100 percent.

If you're thinking of having your delivery at home, think twice, then think again before you leap.

Chapter 26

Tidbits and Tiny Pearls

Grow basil, mint, or parsley in your garden. Their scent will chase the bugs away without your having to use pesticides.

Most expensive vitamins are no better than the cheap ones. Very few drug companies manufacture their own vitamins; most buy from a single source. You're paying for the fancy shape, packaging, and advertising when you buy brand names.

Almost all the aspirin sold in this country is made by the Dow Chemical Co. Paying big prices for aspirin doesn't guarantee getting any better aspirin—it's all acetylsalicylic acid.

Tylenol, aspirin-free Excedrin, and aspirin-free Anacin are all the same drug, namely acetaminophen. Recent animal studies found that a dose slightly larger than standard depressed the immune system by half.

Don't drink large quantities of diet soda. Most contain aspartame (Nutra-sweet). This sweetener goes stale after three months and makes the soda taste bitter. Manufacturers know this, so most add potassium to protect the taste and preserve the freshness. Aspartame is an amino acid and is harmless to humans. Potassium, however, draws calcium from bones, and when taken in large amounts can weaken them. Check the list of contents before you buy.

The cheapest mosquito repellent you can buy is cider vinegar; just spread it on your exposed skin.

From the University of Wisconsin in Madison comes an interesting observation: wooden cutting boards may be safer than plastic ones. In their study, bacteria that cause poisoning in hours disappeared from wooden boards in three minutes, but stayed alive and well on plastic cutting boards after eight hours.

Even the most beautiful woman or handsome man is but four bucketfuls of water and one of salts.

The physician's role as a "patient educator" is not new. The word "doctor" comes from the Latin *docere,* meaning, "to teach," "to lead forth." As early as the fifth century B.C., Hippocrates endorsed this practice.

According to a recent article in *Science* magazine, the mushroom and all humans originated from the same ancestral cell. This conclusion was drawn not by studying the sex lives of humans and mushrooms, but by gene analysis, so all you hardcore vegetarians had better pass on mushrooms or you may be accused of eating a distant relative. As for myself, I'll still order mushrooms on my steak.

Let's have some fun

Write down your house number,
Double it and add five,
Multiply by fifty,
Add your age (don't cheat),
Add 365,
Subtract 615.
What happens? You find your house number at the left and your age at the right.

Here's another

Place twenty-two matches in a single row.
Each player can take one, two, or three matches in each turn.
The key is to always present your opponent with a multiple of four matches.
Begin by taking two, which leaves him with twenty.

Then if he takes one, you take three, leaving him with sixteen; if he takes two, you take two. Repeat this strategy until you leave your opponent with four matches. However many he takes, that last one is yours.

My wife is calling me: "It's time for your nap."

I agree.

Chapter 27

A Vacation In Mexico

It was New Year's Eve; the air was balmy, with scarcely a breeze. A thick slice of moon hung over the Sea of Cortez, illuminating the white sandy beach. Tiny waves in constant rhythm broke gently on the sand and dared to touch our outstretched legs as we lazed supine at the water's edge. "This is about as near to heaven as one can get without being dead," Rob said.

"You must have read my mind," I replied.

"This week has sure gone by fast. I hate to think of going back to work in three more days. You know, Ed, I think I'm getting allergic to kids. Shoot! I can remember when I actually looked forward to going back to school. Now the kids seem so damned spoiled and unruly, I don't care if I ever go back to teaching the brats."

"Yeah, I know how you feel, Rob, but like my boss, old Serge, says, 'Man can't live by dreams alone.'"

"Maybe not, but I'm not sure he needs to work as much as he does. When you boil it down, Ed, what the devil do you work so hard for? Is it money?"

"Of course not. I'm sure you feel pleased and satisfied when your students excel in what you teach. Same as I do when a gal delivers a healthy child after a stormy labor."

"But, is fleeting pleasure and satisfaction reward enough for all the time we've spent? Hell! That's it, Ed—time; *time* is what we want. Look at Pancho: he lives here on the sand in a shack that's just a collection of old wooden crates and cardboard held together by nails and wire, but it keeps the rain out. If you remember, a couple of days ago, I complimented him on the quality of his catch, and asked how long it took him to catch the fish. He replied, 'Not very long, señor.' Then I asked, 'Why don't you stay out longer and catch more... sell more... make a lot of money and buy a bigger boat? You could soon become rich.' 'And after that?' Pancho asked. 'Well, when the business got really good you could start selling stock and make millions!' I replied. 'Millions? Really? And after that?' 'After that you'd be able to retire, live in a tiny village near the coast, sleep late, play with your children, catch a few fish, take siestas, and spend your evenings playing the guitar and singing with your friends.' 'Senor Rob, can't you see that I already have this? I live on the coast, sleep late, and catch just enough fish to satisfy my family. In the evening, I go into the village to see my friends, have a few drinks, and play the guitar and sing a few songs—every day. Why don't you, señor, stay here longer? Why do you have to hurry to get back home when you like it here more?' 'Pancho, I can't answer your question. I don't really know why I'm always in a hurry. You're right, you have it all—it's so simple but so wonderful.'"

"Yes, Rob," I said, "I remember your talk with Pancho very well. It impressed me greatly and made me think. Yet, I'd say that the majority of the people on this earth live simple lives, but I'm sure they're not all happy. I'll grant you, of course, not many are near the sea, nor are they blessed with the good weather Pancho enjoys."

"Yeah, Ed, I know the majority can't help their lot, but you and I are different: we're educated and know the difference; we're fully aware of the opportunity open to us and still are dumb enough to continue our perpetual grind of work. Why do we limit ourselves to just a few days each year to be where we most want to be, and could be, if we chose to?"

"But, Rob, you're forgetting the children. You owe it to them to see that they get a proper education. A good home and the so called necessities of a good life are a must."

"Ed, that's bullshit. Gauguin said, 'Man sacrifices himself for his children, and when they grow up they sacrifice themselves for their children. And so on. As a result everybody sacrifices himself and the lunacy knows no end.'"

"Rob, you're dreaming."

"Not really, Ed. Do you realize Pancho has this every day... *time*—time to enjoy life in the open, the blue sky, the warmth of the sun, and the golden sunset. The sea is his refrigerator, from which he can draw the food he needs. When the tide's out, all he needs to do is wade out and gather all the clams he wants. Tourists like us pay him well to take us out fishing on his dory for just a moment in his life. The money he makes is more than adequate to pay for the groceries and clothing his family needs and the *cerveza* he drinks. Yes, Ed, he has the bountiful life. It's you and I who are the suckers. He is the master of what's most precious to him ... time."

"Rob, you're right, but I'm not sure that it's the way you'd like it. Even if you had it all to do over again, I am sure you'd do the same."

"I don't think so."

"Oh? And what would you have done differently?"

"I think I would teach my children the true meaning of life."

"And what's that?"

"Well, if I had it to do over again ... I might bring them here. I'd want to teach them to work hard and also to play hard. I'd impress upon them that the accumulation of nonessentials has no worth. I'll tell you, Ed, what I mean. Your wife and mine have many dresses, many shoes, many purses, many sets of dishes, and many utensils. There's no way they'll ever wear them out. Yet, if you asked them to part with any, I'm sure they'd argue that they're essential—essential because they set a standard by which to measure against what the Joneses and the Smiths have. But if all of us lost all we had and became bare-assed but healthy, we could and would survive. We'd have to work—it's not easy to live the simple life; it's hard, but Nature is just. There's enough wood, even in this desert-like country, to build a shelter. The sea is bountiful and it wouldn't be long before we'd have a productive garden. Simple food and time to enjoy the real pleasures would be ours all day, every day. We could abandon the thought that we must forgo pleasures now so that in some mythical future we could enjoy the savings we've stored up for a rainy day. There would be no reason to accumulate the nonessentials. Hell! You can't take them with you and at best you can use them only briefly. Our stay on this earth isn't long... so why not enjoy it now? I know it'd be hard work... but hard work, a good sweat, is what makes you feel good. There's nothing invigorating about spending each day, like you do, behind a desk, listening to one complaint after another. Yes, sir, happiness is simple food, a good woman, and a bottle of *cerveza*. Hard work and hard play, all for today."

"Hey, guys, it's New Year's Eve... we want to go into town!"

"O.K., girls, we'll be up in a few minutes," I shouted.

"You know, Rob, we should have washed the dishes for the girls, after they worked so long to prepare that luscious steak dinner. Damn it! We shouldn't have cogitated on the beach so long, especially since it's New Year's Eve."

"Yeah, and convention dictates that we must celebrate, so let's go," Rob replied with loathing.

Our wives were already dressed in multi-colored skirts and stunning blouses, sitting and waiting on the veranda of our rented apartment.

"Be ready in a jiffy, girls," said Rob.

"Guess you and I had better wear those new embroidered shirts the gals bought us yesterday."

"Right, Ed... let's flip to see who gets to shower first."

It was a ten-minute hike into town, over a dirt road. The town, which had no name, consisted of a mini-*super-mercado,* and a small church whose paint had been ravaged by summer storms; even the cement itself had begun to show the ravages of wind and rain. On its front stood a statue of the Virgin Mary, whose poor face was marked by deep pockets of erosion, and the left foot of baby Jesus had crumbled away. There was also a small, dilapidated apartment building, a few homes, a real estate shack, a run-down service station with one gas pump and one old dog, a trailer park, and a big *cantina* so crowded with people that I thought there must be no one left at home.

We had to stand outside the *cantina* to hear the band. In the meantime, Rob worked his way to the bar while we three remained outside, enveloped by the cacophony called music. The ten-piece band played one "rock and roll" song after another.

"I thought we were going to hear Mexican music here in Mexico, not rock and roll," Mable said.

"Maybe they feel that on New Year's Eve they should cater to the large number of Americans here," I answered.

"I love it—at least it's got a Mexican beat," Virginia added.

"What the hell is a Mexican beat?" I asked.

"You know—all that brass and fiddle-de-de; it makes me want to dance. Let's dance, Doc," Virginia said.

"No, thanks," I responded. "Besides, it would be near impossible on this dirt and rock."

Just then Rob returned with four bottles of cold *cerveza.*

"I've never seen a bar so crowded; thought I'd never get in an order...hope you all enjoy my effort."

"Thanks, Rob, we knew you'd get through, and we all appreciate it." I pulled out a *peso* and tossed it to him, "Here's your tip."

"Ouch! Oh, how it hurts!" cried Mable.

"What's the matter?" I asked.

"My finger—it's killing me."

"What did you do?"

"Nothing! I just had my hand behind me and against this brick wall. I wanted to keep my skirt from getting dirty. Oh, God, it hurts!"

"Here, sit down on the ground and let me look at your finger. I can't see anything wrong. Rob, shine your flashlight on her finger. I can't see what could be wrong. Rob, let's look at the wall." In the mortar between two bricks rested a scorpion about an inch and a half long.

"You've been stung by a scorpion, Mable. Let me look at your finger again." I thought I could make out a small puncture mark on the finger, which may have been the entry point for the stinger and where the poison was injected. I used my handkerchief as a tourniquet above the entry point. "Rob, go get some ice cubes from the bar—hurry, please."

The finger was visibly swelling now, and the pain was becoming more excruciating. I took out my pocketknife, showed it to Mable, and said, "Honey, I'm going to make a tiny cut in your finger to get out the venom." She never flinched as I made the stab. I sucked on the wound, but couldn't taste or see any venom. I removed the useless tourniquet. Rob came back with a bag of ice cubes, and a Mexican with his truck followed.

"Señor, I take you all to your house, and I'll pray," the Mexican said.

As soon as we got home I had Mable lie down on the bed, but by now she was so restless from the pain that it was almost impossible to keep her there.

"Mable, please try to keep the ice on your finger. It slows down the absorption of the venom the scorpion injected. Don't worry, dear, scorpion bites in this part of Mexico are nonfatal; it'll hurt, but nothing will happen to you. I'll get you something for the pain."

Rob had already brought my black bag from the car. My brain was racing. I had never treated a scorpion bite in my life; in fact I'd never seen a scorpion. I did recall that in certain areas of Arizona scorpion bites could be fatal, but I think it was only in infants or debilitated patients. Mable was young and healthy—nothing could happen to her, I kept telling myself. I thought she should be given an injection of blood serum that contains specific antitoxin, but that was only available in large medical centers, the nearest of which was 250 miles away in Tucson, Arizona. I recalled that death from scorpion bites was usually caused by respiratory failure, so I couldn't ease her pain with a shot of morphine, as that can depress breathing. I gave her two tablets of Empirin with codeine, quarter-grain, to swallow. After ten minutes she was no better. The pain hadn't let up, so I made her swallow two more of the pills.

Fortunately, Mable's vital signs remained normal. Her pulse was slightly elevated at 100 beats per minute, her blood pressure remained steady at 110/70, and her lungs were working normally at twenty-five breaths per minute.

After another ten minutes, the pain slowly lessened, but was now replaced by hallucinations. Mable kept telling me rats and snakes were trying to bite her. I had a hard time keeping her in bed with me. Her delusions lasted about three or four hours, then gradually subsided, until she fell into a deep sleep. I stayed in bed, holding her close to me all night. I never slept. At seven a.m. she awakened slowly and, thank God, was lucid. I was never so relieved in my life as I was to see her smile and respond sane and well.

It was a hell of a New Year's Eve. I'll never forget it—nor will my darling Mable.

The principal of a fine high school, Rob resigned the very next year; he took early retirement at the age of sixty-two, and was satisfied with a lesser pension than he'd have received had he stayed until he was sixty-five.

Mable and I have visited Rob and Virginia about once a year for the past twenty years, but stay no more than ten days each time. Rob worked hard, and built his own home just a hundred feet above Pancho's shack. He has a large yard loaded with fruit trees, and a garden filled with vegetables. He takes a *siesta* every day; fishes when he feels like it, and sometimes visits his friends in town. Rob and Virginia are happy.

Pancho too made a drastic change, at about the same time Rob did: he left his wife and three girls and never came back. Within a year he became a very busy commercial fisherman, but no one knows what happened to him after that. His wife has moved into town, and his three daughters, who have married, all help their mother.

Who made the right choice—Rob, Pancho, or I?

Chapter 28

Bridge: The Parlor Game

This morning, as I slouch on my eighty-five-year-old buttocks at my desk in the den, I can't help but muse on how forgetful I'm getting.

Last night at bridge, my partner and wife opened with the bid of "one no-trump." I responded promptly and emphatically, "Three no-trump." She passed and proceeded to make "seven no-trump," a "Grand Slam." When we got home, she let me know that I had four aces in my hand. "But that's only sixteen points, and I had no other face cards," I responded.

"You know I opened one no-trump; I had sixteen or more points, my sixteen plus your sixteen for the aces is thirty-two—that's slam range, why didn't you bid it?"

"I don't know," I replied. "I just forgot to add."

Which reminds me now of when and where I first learned to play bridge. It was on New Britain, an island 300 miles long and fifty miles wide that lies off the northeast coast of New Guinea in the South Pacific. The year was 1943; the Japanese controlled most of New Britain, and let us know by bombing us almost every day and night. My friend and "foxhole neighbor" was a psychiatrist from Philadelphia. Before the war, he had won the Pennsylvania State Bridge Championship. "Would you like me to teach you to play bridge?" he shouted from his hole in the ground.

"Sure would, Hirsh." I always called him that; his last name was Hirshfield.

Bridge is really a simple game that you can learn to play in a day. I did. But once you do, you can spend a lifetime getting good at it. It requires an agile, analytic mind, immense memory, and intense concentration. It's burdened by innumerable systems and conventions. Somerset Maugham, a physician, famous writer, and excellent bridge player once said, "I could never hope to remember all the rules, and to do so would only confuse me; I stick to no more than six and common sense." He also said, "Bridge is the most entertaining and intelligent card game the wit of man has so far devised."

Today, bridge is the most fiercely competitive game you can play while sitting on your derriere. If you make a mistake in bidding, and especially if you compound it with an error in play, you are in for a battle royal. It happened in a husband/wife bridge game in Kansas, and when they got home, she shot and killed him for it!

Bridge has been blamed for deep-seated hostility, divorce, and murder. It's a stressful game, but I don't think it can be blamed for killing, divorce, or ill-tempered outbursts. People who can't handle stress in bridge will crack under any type of stress they experience, and probably shouldn't play bridge.

Ely Culbertson and Charles Goren get credited for today's type of bridge play, but there are at least twelve other bridge champions who contributed to its creation. The Russians claim the credit should belong to them, since both Culbertson and Goren had Russian blood flowing in their arteries.

Ely (Ilya) Culbertson was born in Poijana de Verbilao, Romania, in the summer of 1893. His father was born in the United States of Scotch descent. His mother, Xenia Rogozny, was born in Russia; she was the daughter of a Cossack chief. Ely spent his youth in a Cossack village in central Russia. He spoke Russian and hated school. His older brother, Eugene, became a monk. His two sisters died in childhood, and his other brother, Sasha, born in 1895, became a famous violinist. Ely did poorly in school, and almost chose to go to a monastery and become "the greatest saint on earth," he said. But he soon changed his mind and decided to become a rebel. He got into a fight over a woman and landed in jail. There he developed a hunger to read both Russian and English. He resolved to become a writer and did write a book—about a man who believed his buttocks were made of precious stones. The book was never was accepted for publication.

By this time, his father had become very wealthy from his oil business, and Ely, like many wealthy kids, couldn't find what he really wanted to do. He became interested in the problems of the poor peasants and hard-pressed workers. He took part in a large community demonstration that was broken up by the famous horse-riding Cossacks (the so-called Czar's Marines). Many people were killed. (Later, these same Cossacks massacred my father's family.)

Soon after the horrible riot, Ely fell in love with Nadya, a beautiful student revolutionist. He joined the Communist Party. In the next communist demonstration, the Cossacks killed Nadya. While trying to avenge her death, Ely was arrested and put in jail. He could have died there, but his mother's influence secured his release—after all, she was the daughter of the Cossack chief.

After his release from jail, Ely's father sent him to America to get educated at Yale. Again, he hated school, and soon left Yale. He went to Canada to work as a timekeeper at a labor camp; he was fired for trying to organize the workers. He left for Mexico and tried to join the revolutionists there, but failed, so he tried his luck in Geneva, where he first learned to play auction bridge and resolved to become the "world's best." At this time he also adopted the young daughter of a French prostitute.

In the Russian Revolution of 1917, Ely's father lost all his possessions and money. He took Ely and his brother, Sasha, to America. All three were penniless. In New York, Ely kept them clothed and fed by winning at bridge. He soon got access to the Knickerbockers Whist Club, where his winnings increased dramatically. There he met Josephine Dillon, a good-looking young widow who happened to be America's greatest woman bridge player. They married in 1923 and had two children, Joyce Nadya and Bruce Ely.

Ely worked hard and long to become the best in contract

bridge. At this time, Josephine, his wife, was always his partner in bridge. In 1925, American yachtsman Harold S. Vanderbilt and other expert auction bridge players created contract bridge while on a long cruise. But it was Ely who, in 1930, wrote the *Contract Blue Book* in two frantic weeks. It became an enormous success. Later the book summary, written entirely by his wife, sold even better. They became world-famous and rich, and then almost lost it all when Ely decided to go into the business of making plastic cards.

He went deep into debt, but by winning in high-stakes bridge games, held out until he was able to sell the card-making business for a huge profit; with the money he built a grand mansion in New York. Soon Ely became nervous and depressed, fought with Josephine, and they divorced. However, they continued to live together, he on one floor and she on the other. They also continued to play bridge together and shared its profits.

Ely enjoyed needling his bridge opponents, and fancied himself an invincible gambler. He himself said, "I work day and night to be brilliant. By nature, damn cocky, not really *very* cocky, but cocky."

He lived well, keeping an expensive suite in New York and an estate in Ridgefield, Connecticut. At dinner he dressed fashionably, and always mixed his own salad dressing. No dinner was complete unless accompanied by caviar, goose liver, and vintage wines. He spoke six languages fluently, each with a distinct Russian accent. A resentful competitor once remarked, "One either likes Mr. Culbertson or abhors him; there is no middle ground."

Ely died in 1955 at the age of sixty-two.

Charles Henry Goren was born in Philadelphia in March of 1901 to Jacob and Rebecca, Russian-born Jewish immigrants. He was as different from Culbertson as day from night. Women loved him, and he never provoked his opponents. "After all," he said, "they may someday buy my books." He did well in school and, in 1923, got his law degree at McGill University in Montreal, but he did poorly practicing law—he admitted he never made more than $5,000 a year at it.

Goren started playing bridge for money while a student at McGill. He bought Milton C. Work's *Auction Bridge,* and absorbed it completely. Later, Goren actually got a job ghost-writing Work's daily bridge column, for which Mr. Work paid him thirty-five dollars a week. Determined to master the game, he soon began winning local tournaments, but could see that the big money was in teaching and writing about bridge. He quit playing for money and gave up the practice of law. His first book, *Winning Bridge Made Simple,* was published in 1936. It was an amalgam, mixing Culbertson's honor trick method with Milton Work's point counting. In revised editions he made minor changes, but in 1951, in Goren's *New Contract Bridge Complete,* he abandoned all of Culbertson's system and stuck mostly to Work's point system.

In 1955 Goren himself reported that it was selling 1,000 copies a day and had been translated into several foreign languages. Altogether, he wrote over forty books on bridge, plus a weekly column on bridge for *Sports Illustrated,* and appeared on TV teaching bridge. As far as I know, he remained a bachelor, and his principal bridge partner was Mrs. Helen Sobel, a one-time chorus girl. He loved to play golf and attend the theater and symphony. In his younger years he was a chain cigar smoker. He was much in demand socially, and his bridge partners included many famous people, including Somerset Maugham. On April 12, 1991, Goren died in Encino, California, at the age of ninety.

Bridge has been described by a former champion as a form of mental warfare, whether playing for high stakes or merely for "blood."

There are many coded or artificial ways to help you tell your partner how to respond to your original bid. However you must tell your *opponents* of any coded or artificial bids you use. For example, my saying "one club" means I have three or less clubs and want you, my partner to name your four-card major suit.

If you don't have it, then bid "one diamond." Another example you can use is a "reverse" bid, in which, for tactical reasons, you place a given contract in your partner's hand by bidding "four diamonds." This instructs your partner to bid the next highest suit; thus you arrive at a four-heart partnership contract you really want. You can vary the type of reverse bidding in so many ways that it can literally drive you nuts. Personally, I detest the system. Or, you can cheat by secret signals with your fingers, a significant look, word, or gesture. All these rules, conventions, systems, and gestures will eventually open the door for you to the "parlor war." Somerset Maugham was right when he advocated sticking to no more than six rules and common sense.

I'll close with an old tale from which I still get a good belly laugh. A cleaning woman was applying for a new position. When asked why she'd left her last place, she replied, "Oh, the pay was good, but it was the dirtiest place I've worked in. They played a game called bridge, and last night there were a lot of people in the parlor. As I was about to bring in the refreshments, I heard a man say, 'Lay down and let's see what you got.' Another man said to a lady, 'I got strength, but no length,' and another man said to a lady, 'Take your hands off my trick!' Well, I pert near dropped dead! Just then the lady answered, 'You forced me. You jumped me twice, when you didn't have the strength for one raise.' Another woman was talking about protecting her honor. Well, I just picked up my hat and coat and, as I was leaving, I hope to die, if one of them didn't say, 'Well, I guess we'll go home now; that was the last rubber.'"

Chapter 29

Guilt and Pain

Both guilt and pain are essential elements of life; if they weren't, life would be hell on earth.

Guilt is the feeling we experience when we do wrong and know it. We regard it with extreme repugnance because it affects what we do. It makes absolutely no difference whether you believe in God or not—you feel guilt; it plays a major part in what you say and do.

However, there are people who continue to do wrong and even kill. Their brains don't contain guilt receptors. We don't know how to change them, so we incarcerate or execute them.

Pain is equally necessary and important. For example, in my first years of practice, a mother brought her two-year-old son into my office. His right hand was wrapped in a large, icy, wet towel. The boy greeted me with a smile and was in no visible discomfort. The mother was in agony: tears were flowing down her cheeks; she could hardly say, "He burned his hand on the stove."

I had the boy sit down, brought my chair near to him, and slowly removed the towel. The palm of his hand looked like it was charbroiled. "Does it hurt?" I asked.

"No," he replied. I couldn't believe what I was looking at.

I asked his mother, "Has he ever complained of pain?"

"Not that I know of," she answered.

"Did you see him burn his hand?"

Teeth chattering, she replied, "I just took a kettle of boiling water off the stove and set in on the sink and began pouring the water into a larger container when I noticed he was standing on his tiptoes with his right hand on the hotplate of the stove. I screamed and dashed to the stove and removed his hand. It didn't seem to hurt him at all. I could see his hand was burned very badly, so I soaked a big towel in ice water, wrapped his hand, and came right here. I just live on the next street."

With the mother's permission, I hospitalized the boy and referred him to a plastic surgeon. He received extensive treatment and several surgeries. He didn't lose his hand, but it was scarred for life and he probably never regained full use of it. I don't know what happened to this boy, because they moved a few weeks later—I never knew where.

Can you imagine how careful he had to be for the rest of his life? He had to live without warning from pain; he could get seriously ill and not know it; he could have died from some simple, easily curable malady that was never brought to his attention by pain—because he had no pain receptors in his brain.

Guilt is a warning in the same way that pain acts as a red flag when your tooth is abscessed or your appendix inflamed. Ignore guilt or pain and you're headed for disaster. You must listen to guilt feelings and cease doing things that give rise to them. Remember, guilt is your ally, not your enemy: it's trying to set you straight; listen to it. Believe it or not, you do have a conscience and it's telling you whether you do right or wrong. The guilty feeling you get is its byproduct. Be thankful you have both guilt and pain.

> *"The trouble with the world is that the stupid are cocksure and the intelligent full of doubt."*
>
> —Bertrand Russell

Chapter 30

People Are No Damned Good

One day, long ago, on an island in the southwest Pacific, my surgical team and I, exhausted, sat down to rest in the shade of some battle-scarred palm trees. The chaplain walked up and handed each of us a sheet of paper. On it was a drawing of a sad-eyed, forlorn man, sitting with his legs crossed, cramped in a small cage where he had isolated himself to escape the realities of the world. The caption under it read People Are No Damned Good. At that moment, the chaplain couldn't have expressed my feelings more vividly, because I was tired of war and all its carnage.

Now, sixty years and two wars later, this country is beset by a multitude of protests and social unrest. Almost daily, new assaults are directed against our way of life. It's easy again to picture oneself as the man in the cage, threatened by all those people who are no damned good.

The young, full of energy and disillusioned by the present state of affairs, are impatient and demanding of change. Just recently, a bright graduate student expressed his thoughts and feelings to me as follows: "You of the old order have a simplistic view of the world. You find comfort and justify your position in life by declaring that those in penury deserve to be there. The poor and needy, the unfortunate fellow man whom you piously pity in church twice a year, is always a member of India or South America's starving masses, for whom you gratefully cough up a few nickels and dimes. The poor at home, however, are poor because they're too lazy to get off their duffs and work for a living. You always ascribe to them negative characteristics: drunkenness, laziness, and licentiousness, etc. You say they breed too much, don't marry, and are dirty and uncouth. Your mania to preserve the status quo, often at any cost, leads to the kind of thinking that refuses to recognize ambiguity or complexity, the sort of thinking that pigeonholes things into stereotypes."

His criticism was sharp and direct, and had elements of truth. However, he offered no constructive solutions. He too was guilty of stereotyping, and was the man in the box as well.

It doesn't tax our gray matter very much to be destructively critical. An emotional outburst is all it takes to hurt someone. If we are to get out of the box and stop seeing people as "no damned good," it's essential that we understand them, know their limitations and weaknesses, and be willing to help them instead of using them as steppingstones to our success.

Each of us is a complex mass of protoplasm charged with hate, love, doubt, fear, and anger. These emotions are necessary for self-preservation and to satisfy our needs and desires. The jackass is similarly endowed; we differ from animals primarily in that we are capable of reasoning, and should therefore be held responsible for our conduct. When we abdicate responsibility and give vent to our emotions, we invite trouble. We're all familiar with the compulsive neurotic who constantly complains and seeks medication. It's impossible for him to consider that, through the unbridled exercise of fear, he alone is responsible for his predicament. It's easier for him to seek relief for his symptoms through drugs than it is to admit that he's to blame. The drunk on the freeway, the addict with the gun, the mob in the street, are all acting on emotions severed from responsibility. We can evaluate the entire spectrum of human behavior by the degree of responsibility that motivates it.

Today, responsibility is shunned at all levels: parents relegate the discipline of their children to teachers or psychiatrists; executives appoint a committee when problems arise; young and old use drugs and alcohol to stimulate, jollify, or pacify. Anything is all right, as long as it frees one of responsibility for seeing things as they really are. The joy of work is dying, and the prime accent in life seems to be on the pursuit of pleasure. Some of our children fancy themselves composers, artists, or writers, thinking these endeavors can be pursued with little work or skill. Any sound, as long as it's loud and repetitive, is considered music, and sold as an experience. Many a painting displayed as creative expression is in reality a product of unbridled emotions splashed onto canvas by incompetents or fakers. Is it any wonder that a monkey's paintings have won prizes? Sex, with all its variations and unrestricted emotional garble, is the fashion and formula for successful writing. Skill and order is hard to find in today's artistic offerings; responsible conduct is even less apparent, but we can't blame the young alone for the desertion of responsibility, because we induced it. We reared a generation according to the premise that to deny is harmful and wicked, and to discipline is to hinder. We showered our children with things to love, but denied them our own love and understanding.

We set our goals toward economic gain and devoted most of our time and energy to it. In our haste to build this rich and powerful nation, we exploited the undeveloped countries and polluted our air, land, and water. As a result, we now witness conduct that shocks us: we're alarmed by the riots in the streets and angered by disturbances on the campuses; we can't comprehend why some want this system overthrown.

There is an urgent need to create order from chaos. The answer, however, isn't in replacing our system with another, for the fault is not in our system but in its people. Once a society becomes wholly dedicated to economic development and exploitation, it can't help but reduce the stature of its people and destroy the natural beauty of its country. It's time each of us developed an awareness of our shortcomings.

We must alleviate poverty; find jobs for the employable, and foster responsibility if we are to avoid a second revolution. Our government is well aware of the problems and is making efforts to solve them, but it needs help from all its citizens.

Reform won't come from those who protest most and loudest, for they are seldom constructively oriented, and, not infrequently, are selfishly motivated or directed by a power resolved to destroy us.

Each year our government spends additional billions to eliminate poverty and create new jobs. This spending has the support of many business and financial leaders. Many plans have been proposed to eliminate poverty: Negative Income Tax, Income Allowance Plan, Economic Security Plan, Family Security Program, and others. All stress a guaranteed income one way or another, but offer little more. Occasionally, a bit of effort is directed toward building initiative and fostering responsibility. In the meantime, you and I are paying for these experiments in "compensation without participation." The jobs that are created are mostly stopgaps against some current upheaval; these jobs are frequently useless and of the "dead-end" variety, that is, they're not really necessary, and offer little chance for advancement or hope of security.

We won't solve the ills of this country by giving gifts, no matter how disguised, to the unemployed. It's a poor measure of a man or country to expect gratitude, respect, and order by this method. It's equally degrading to the man who constantly accepts favors, because it only makes him conscious of being a second-rate citizen. Such methods are used for household pets, not humans. The answer to poverty also doesn't lie in further crippling conscientious and industrious workers. It's time our government gave them a pat on the back for a job well done instead of further weighing them down with increased taxes.

It is with this interplay of emotions and ideas that I would like to propose a plan, albeit in embryonic form, with the hope that some among you may find enough merit in it to adopt it and make it grow.

My plan is to establish a sabbatical: for each continuous six years of work, each employee would receive one year of vacation with full pay. The concept of a sabbatical is not new—the ancient

Hebrews, according to Mosaic Law, allowed the land to remain fallow every seventh year, the purpose being to rejuvenate the land. Man needs rejuvenation even more.

According to recently published government statistics, there are now 77.3 million Americans employed, while 3.6 million are without jobs. If one-sixth of the labor force of 77.3 million were on sabbatical, we would have nearly 13 million jobs available—useful, meaningful jobs with built-in steps for advancement.

To begin, our government could choose depressed areas where the need is most urgent. It could then assign certain industries, to which it contributes the bulk of its orders, to initiate this program. Averaged out, the cost would be no greater than if a four-day working week were adopted, for which there is now a movement. Funds for the sabbatical could be established by having the employer sacrifice some profit and by having the government do its part through direct subsidies and compensatory tax incentives to the employer.

Not everyone with six years of continuous employment could walk off the job at the same time or utter chaos would occur. Before a sabbatical could be granted to any employee, it would first be his responsibility to participate actively in the program by teaching the uneducated and inexperienced applicant the intricacies of his job through an expanded form of apprenticeship. An equitable system of eligibility could be evolved by bringing into play some type of point system based on merit, and dependent on the apprentice's ability to perform the particular job.

If this plan were adopted, it would require an economic counterbalance of some sort, since, with millions on vacation, a great demand for help would be created in the entertainment and service fields. However, if we are to believe that automation will progressively eliminate more jobs, then this changeover to jobs within the service and entertainment fields may be the solution we will need later to prevent a new wave of unemployment.

My prime purpose for proposing the sabbatical plan is to create jobs for the employable, but I would also hope that for those on sabbatical it would become a time for self-reevaluation and re-identification. In this changing world, everything is rapidly becoming more complex, and it's easy to develop feelings of helplessness and irresponsibility. It's difficult for the individual worker to maintain a feeling of responsibility for his work when he often doesn't even recognize what his contribution adds to the final product. Too often the life of the working person turns into one of monotony and confinement. In believing he can buy happiness and love, he surrounds himself and his family with material things. The more he buys, the deeper in debt he goes, and, as a result, he frequently comes home from work worried, tired, and is ill tempered, and neither wants to listen to trivia, nor be burdened with the responsibility of his children. The confinement and commitment become so real and fatiguing that, all too often, they lead to the breakup of the home.

Our youngsters sense our inability to transcend the mere making of money, and believe we derive little joy from work. They find our kind of life dull and unrewarding, and say we've lost our identities in the material things we surround ourselves with. They rebel, and cry out for the simple life; they say we no longer care for each other, have long rejected them, and are hell-bent for destruction. Perhaps it's time we took notice of what they say.

We can't stop progress and go back to the simple life, but we could use the sabbatical year to rejuvenate our lives and restore family life. Children should be excused from school in the year of their parents' sabbaticals to be able to travel, work, learn, and play with them. Travel across this country and in foreign lands would increase as never before. Foreign visitors could see for themselves that there are other Americans besides millionaires, lowbrows, and racists.

Some on sabbatical might decide to go back to school, join the Peace Corps, work on farms or in hospitals, hire out on ships, work in politics, assist the poor, educate the illiterate, train the unskilled, or do a little of each.

We could once again choose the life we want to live. We could all have the opportunity to become activists like the pioneers who opened up this country, rather than the armchair passivists that we are, trying to hold on to a way of life that can't persist. I know no better way to close than by paraphrasing Alexis Zorba, the Greek: "You have everything...but one thing...madness! A man needs a little madness to cut the rope and be free."

Chapter 31

Old Age

When is one old? It depends on how you define it. Some are old at fifty, and content to spend the rest of their lives in a rocking-chair existence—not because they're sick or disabled, they just prefer to sit on their butts.

Others remain active deep into their nineties and over. Not too long ago, Bob Hope and George Burns danced together on TV. Both were in their nineties. Though you might not appreciate either one's acting, you can't help admiring them for doing it. Neither needs the money. They continue to perform because they thrive on it, and know that they're bringing relaxation and laughter to others.

Barring accidents and disease, age is really a process of wear and tear. You are largely responsible for how fast this occurs. The French author André Maurois said it well when he remarked, "Growing old is no more than a bad habit which a busy man has no time to form."

During the height of the Cold War, Conrad Adenauer served with vigor as chancellor of West Germany until the age of eighty-seven.

Edwin Parker, M.D.

There is something special to be learned from the life of Harry Nohr, who, in 1962, at age sixty-five, retired as postmaster of a small town in Wisconsin. He could have taken his place in "the easy life," but chose instead to work with lathe and chisel. Combing the hills of southwestern Wisconsin, Nohr located the best wood he could find—his creations are highly sought after by museums and private collectors. When asked his secret for finding these remarkable woods, he answered, "It's always the tree that's been stressed and challenged, and surviving in a high windy place, that yields the wood I value most."

So it is with life.

One in every seven of us in the United States is over sixty-five. Within ten years there will be about 100,000 over 100 years old.

After seventy years our bodies slow down: it takes us longer to get up and down; we notice changes in our hearing and vision, but let's be careful not to exaggerate these losses. Arthritis can be helped with medication and surgery. Many develop cataracts, but these can be removed. Older people may start to lose their ability to hear high tones, but as a rule they don't become deaf. Often the problem has more to do with concentration than disease. You all know people who can't hear a thing until you whisper—that's called "selective hearing." They hear the whispering because their concentration is entirely on hearing what you say; they've laid aside their own anxieties for the moment.

Memory loss is a great concern of the elderly. When a fifteen-year-old forgets where he put his shoes, nobody gives a damn, but if you're over sixty, look out—you're going to be labeled with Alzheimer's or senility.

There are three kinds of memory:

1. *Episodic, or recall on demand*
   a. *The clerk asks your phone number and you can't remember.*
   b. *You meet someone on the street, you recognize her, but can't remember her name.*

If you relax, you will in time recall the phone number and the woman's name. This demand (episodic) memory is the only one that declines with age.

2. *Implicit memory, which lets us use language and other skills. It stays the same. For example, you don't forget to speak, drive a car, read a book, watch a movie, or play an instrument.*
3. *Semantic memory, which is the internal computer in which we've stored all our years of experience and information, and upon which we draw to make judgments and decisions. The seat of wisdom, this memory continues to grow. It is this semantic memory that allows the elderly to recall distant events so clearly.*

The old are great storytellers. The young are always in a hurry, and few find time to listen. The old sense this, and, as a result, lose self-esteem. Add to this their aches and pains, the loss of a spouse and/or best friend, and loss of sensory perception and mobility, and perhaps you can understand their predicament. It seems easiest to place them in homes for the aged.

So, if you do live long enough to become "old" and disabled, try to remember what Thomas Carlyle said: "Work is the grand cure for all the maladies and miseries that ever beset mankind." It may help keep you out of the home for the aged. The physical work can be no more than learning to paint a picture or write your autobiography. Your children will love it, and if you never sell a book—so what?

Chapter 32

How to Become an M.D.

The formula is simple. It takes no special talent to become a doctor of medicine. To reach this goal you need to be:

1. *Determined, meaning, you'll settle for nothing less;*
2. *Persistent, meaning, come hell or high water, you won't change your mind.*

To put this formula into practice, however, you must:

1. *Learn to enjoy work.*
2. *Be willing and able to forestall worldly pleasures.*
3. *Remember always to keep your nose to the grindstone!*

This requires *discipline,* which means you choose what you do; you are your own boss. For example, when you have the urge to turn on the TV, you choose instead to open a textbook and study. When the phone rings and you're invited to a party, you elect to decline and get back to your homework. In time, it will become clear that each time you say no to a diversion or a pleasure and instead, by free choice, choose to work, you're getting closer to your reward—the M.D. degree.

On a hot California afternoon almost thirty-five years ago, I was in the stands with Stan Smith's father. His son had just won the Pasadena City Junior Championship in tennis. Beaming with joy, Stan ran up to where we were sitting and hugged his dad. Equally overjoyed, his father congratulated him enthusiastically. However, after a short interval he said, "Son, you won, and I'm happy for you, but you played poorly. Now you must give up golf, pool, basketball, swimming, and carousing. From now on, you're going to concentrate on tennis only!"

As you may know, Stan Smith became a world champion tennis player and won at Wimbledon. He still plays a damn good game of tennis. Stan's dad gave him the formula for success; Stan chose to follow it. That's discipline—and its reward.

Why Do You Want to Be a Doctor?

In my case, it was "natural"—my uncle was a country doctor. I made house calls with him in his model-A Ford. I thought no one on earth knew as much as he did. I watched him perform miracles; I just had to be a doctor—there was no other choice for me.

Perhaps you were fascinated by a movie you saw in which a pediatrician, by skill and devotion, saves the life of a baby who weighed just one and half pounds at birth. Or the reruns of *MASH,* where for the third or fourth time you watched in awe as Captain Hawkins put back together the shrapnel-shattered body of a young G.I—you just knew Hawkins wouldn't let him die. Or the obstetrician who, in the nick of time, delivered a baby by Caesarean section, saving two lives at once—the mother, who was bleeding to death from a torn placenta and the baby, who was being choked to death by lack of oxygen. Who said only Jesus performs miracles?

Most doctors aren't rich, and not one has ever performed a miracle—including my uncle. All the unusual and fascinating events you see on TV and in movies are made possible only by long study and hard work. They are strictly accomplishments, not supernatural acts. An accomplishment is often deceptive, because we don't see the pain and perseverance that produced it. It's so much simpler for the uninformed to call it a miracle.

Where and How Do You Start Preparing Yourself for Medical School?

High school is a good place to start, but it's even better to begin in elementary school. The sooner you learn to discipline yourself and work hard, the easier your task. The grades you get in high school will determine whether the door to higher education will be opened to you or slammed in your face. Good grades are an absolute prerequisite for entrance to college. A GPA of 3.5 or better in college is a *sine qua non* for admission to medical school.

You and I might not agree that good grades should play so important a part in determining who goes to college, but that's the way it is. Until someone comes up with a better way to determine who is qualified, it will remain so. Good grades aren't that hard to come by if you apply yourself honestly and diligently to the work. In fact, it can be fun. Believe me, you're in for a great thrill when you bring home a "straight-A" report card—and you'll never forget the expression on Mom's and Dad's faces when they see all those A's.

What Does It Cost in Time and Money to Get an M.D. Degree?

- *Eight years of elementary school*
- *Four years of high school*
- *Four years of college*
- *Four years of medical school*
- *One year of internship*
- *Total: twenty-one years of education*

On average, you start elementary school at age six, therefore you're twenty-seven before you can practice medicine. If you decide to specialize, add another three to five years of residency. This means that you'll be over thirty before you can start work in your chosen field. Your high school friends will already be established in their respective fields, and probably saving money while you are, in all probability, heavily in debt.

Is It Worth It?

You bet your life it is. When my wife and I look back on my medical school, internship, and residency years, we realize they were the most happy and exciting years of our lives. We met when I was a freshman medical student. We purposely delayed our marriage until I had my sheepskin in hand. We married forty-eight hours later in the university church, and have lived together for over half a century. The challenges in practicing medicine, then and now, are ever present and the rewards plentiful. Would I do it again? *Absolutely,* and exactly the same way!

Money?

It takes a lot. You may be fortunate enough to have parents who help you financially. If you don't, there are ways open to get an M.D. degree. The United States government offers scholarships in three services: army, navy and air force. Apply to all three—you improve your odds of being accepted. You can get full information by writing to the following military departments:

For the army, address correspondence to:
Commander, U.S. Army Health Professional
Support Agency SGPS - PDF
5109 Leesbury Pike
Falls Church, VA 22041-3258
You can write directly to the army's medical school:
Director of Admissions
Uniformed Services University of the Health Sciences
4301 Jones Bridge Rd.
Bethesda, MD 20814-4799

For the navy write to:
Commander, Navy Recruiting Command
4015 Wilson Blvd.
Arlington, VA 22203

For the air force write to:
U.S. Air Force Recruiting Services
Directorate of Health Professionals

Medical Recruiting Division
Randolph Air Force Base, TX 78150-5421

If accepted, you're immediately placed on active duty: you receive officer's pay and benefits; you pay no tuition, and get free housing and food. You'll be given full details when you inquire.

If government service doesn't interest you, there are other ways to get help:

1. *Most state and private medical schools offer scholarships. Write to the dean of the school of your choice.*
2. *Government loans are available to the needy and disadvantaged. Write to the director of financial aid at the school you're applying to.*

Disadvantaged students can also obtain scholarships from government-sponsored agencies such as NHSC (National Health Service Corp.). Current information may be had by writing to:

NHSC Scholarship Program
Parklawn Bldg., Room 7-29
5600 Fishers Lane
Rockville, MD 20857

Or call (301) 443-1650. If you're short on stamps or coins, you can listen to a recorded announcement that will give you details for applying for a medical school scholarship. Call toll-free (800) 638-0824. You can call day or night. Don't procrastinate—go for it!

3. *Part-time work is available for those who have some means, but not enough.*

I worked as an attendant on the wards of the St. Louis Insane Asylum, in St. Louis, Missouri, from six p.m. to midnight, six days a week, for all my four years at medical school. Most of the patients were asleep by eight p.m., so I had ample time to study and was seldom disturbed. For this I received free room, board, and laundry, plus twenty dollars a month. In addition, I worked the lunch hour in the medical school library, sorting and returning books to their proper places for one hour each school day. For this the federal government paid me thirty dollars a month—in the 1930s that was great pay!

There are just as many or more jobs available to the student today:

1. *Sanitariums, hospitals, and rest homes are begging for night attendants.*
2. *House-sitting jobs are available (put an ad in the local newspaper—you'll be surprised at the response).*
3. *You can run errands for the disabled.*
4. *Fast-food restaurants are always looking for help in the evenings—they even feed you!*

These are but a few possibilities; I'll bet you can think of a lot more opportunities to make a few extra dollars.

In closing, let me suggest that in choosing a college, you pick one that has a medical school on its campus. This gives you opportunities to see and talk to the members of the medical school admissions committee. It also allows them time to evaluate your abilities and acceptability for medical school. If you choose a college very distant from the nearest medical school, your chances of getting accepted to medical school dwindle in a hurry. Eye-to-eye contact and verbal communication beats the hell out of letter writing.

When in college, apply early to the medical school of your choice, preferably in your freshman year, and no later than your sophomore year. Don't get discouraged if you're rejected; there are a lot of medical schools—keep trying. Ask your family doctor for his advice. Seek out a retired doctor in your town; I'm sure he'll gladly do all he can to help you get into medical school—assuming you have the scholastic qualifications.

You can do it. In 1936, in my freshman year at St. Louis University School of Medicine, I had a classmate, a lawyer, who was forty-five years old. After twenty years practicing law he had become bored with it. It took three years of trying before he was accepted to medical school. He proudly showed anyone who was interested a crateful of rejection letters from almost every medical school in the United States and Canada. He graduated near the top of our class, and went on to practice medicine for twenty-five years before retiring.

Your local library will get you a list of all the U.S. and Canadian medical schools, their addresses, names of the deans, tuitions charged, and much more. The *Journal of the American Medical Association* also lists this information. I haven't suggested foreign schools because I know so little about them. Suffice to say, there are no scholarships available to them, and in most cases you must be able to speak the language. It's important to know that getting an M.D. degree from a foreign medical school doesn't automatically allow you to practice medicine in the United States or Canada. You'll have to take special examinations, and might have to take further schooling in the United States. It's prudent to speak to a foreign graduate who is now practicing in America for details before deciding to go to a foreign school.

Now get off your posterior and lay out your plans. Learn to enjoy work and put your nose to the grindstone. Don't buy the "bull" that hard work produces stress and deprives you of time for fun. Time is plentiful when you're young—it's only when you get old that there aren't enough hours in the day.

Remember that there are two types of stress, bad and good. Bad stress is tension, which is used to do a job or task you hate, detest, or don't give a damn for. It can contribute to an early heart attack. Good stress is mental force used to do a job you enjoy and know you'll be rewarded for. Stick with good stress—it can only make you feel good. Show what you're made of; exercise a little intestinal fortitude. You can make it!

Good luck!

Section Two

Chapter 1

Happiness

Have you ever asked yourself, "What makes one person happy throughout his life and another content to plod through it, reciting an endless litany of misfortune, distress, and pain?" I'm sure you have, and I'm equally certain the answers are familiar to you. Leading every list for attaining happiness have always been:

1. Good health,

2. Wealth, and

3. Fame.

But these answers are *wrong!*

Robert Louis Stevenson was so desperately ill and weakened by repeated lung hemorrhages that he had to do most of his writing in bed. Yet, he gave the world *Treasure Island* and a priceless legacy of prose and inspiring essays. Allow me to quote a piece he wrote before he died of an exsanguinating hemorrhage in 1894 at the age of forty-four.

The Gallant Life

It is better to lose health like a spendthrift than to waste it like a miser. It is better to live and be done with it, than to die daily in the sickroom. By all means begin your folio; even if the doctor does not give you a year, even if he hesitates about a month, make one brave push and see what can be accomplished in a week. It is not only in finished undertakings that we ought to honor useful labor.... All who have meant good work with their whole hearts have done good work, although they may die before time to sign it. Every heart that has beat strong and cheerfully has left a hopeful impulse behind it in the world and bettered the tradition of mankind.

—Robert Louis Stevenson

A young woman who lived not far from me was born with rudimentary limbs: her lower extremities ended above the middle of the thighs; she had stumps for arms. As a child, her brother taught her to propel herself by sliding on her bottom. By age five she could write by holding a pencil between her chin and shoulder. When she learned to use an electric wheelchair a whole new world opened up for her. She graduated from college with honors and was elected to Phi Beta Kappa. She studied for a year in Paris, where she had to climb four flights on her bottom to her classroom, losing ten pounds in the process. Her only comment was, "It was great, 'cause I could eat all the pastries I wanted to!" She worked, wrote, and dated, yet she required help for all the routine things we take for granted, such as eating, dressing, and bathroom needs. A very bright and cheerful person, she has often been quoted as saying, "I have little tolerance for the handicapped who say, 'Poor me.'"

Remember the good-looking Canadian whose leg was amputated because of cancer. He promised to run across the entire length of Canada on his remaining leg to raise a million dollars for cancer research. He only made it halfway, forced to stop because he could not breathe, the cancer was filling his lungs.

He raised over $20 million.

The painter, Renoir, was so crippled by arthritis that friends had to tape his brushes to his fingers. He painted that way till he died.

Ray Charles is blind, yet is one of our top entertainers. Hemingway was a famous writer; still he blew his head off. J. Paul Getty, one of the wealthiest men on earth, was most unhappy.

So, if good health, wealth, and fame do not guarantee happiness, what does? How do you find it? "Dear Abby" might tell us to talk to psychologists; after all, that's their specialty. We might not like their answer. Most have been saying the same thing for centuries: "The way to be truly happy is to serve others." Then why aren't most people happy? After all, the majority of us work, so we serve somebody.

"True," say the psychologists, "but that's not enough. First you must realize that you are useful and necessary and that you are fully aware of the result of your work." That is not always easy, but it can be done. There's an old story about two bricklayers working at opposite ends of a wall. An old man was watching, and his curiosity was aroused, so he walked over to one of them and asked what he was doing. The worker turned, muttered a few cuss words, and said, "What the hell do you think I'm doing—I'm laying bricks!" The elderly man thanked him and walked over to the other worker, who was whistling as he tapped a freshly laid brick into place. He asked him the same question. "Sir," the man replied, "I'm helping build a beautiful cathedral on this corner." Now, that's what the psychologists mean when they say you must develop a healthy attitude to build up your self-respect and get on the road to happiness.

Some time ago I read an article by a very wise man warning us not to hurry through life. He suggested that on short errands we walk instead of using our cars. "Take the train instead of a plane whenever you can. Use the country roads instead of the interstate freeways. Take time to look out the window, to smell the roses. Life should be sipped, not gulped," he said, "it should be savored for the love and kindness and happiness there is in it—for the beauty and goodness and opportunities it holds."

Naturally, those rewards are hard to come by when you're working and preoccupied with a tight schedule. But be honest with yourself, deep down, you know you can always fit some of these ideas into your schedule.

"Don't just dash through life and try to gobble up as much as you can before the platter is taken away. That's not life's purpose—you can't take it with you—we are not here to Get, but to Become," he concluded.

> *"The art of loving is like all arts; it must be learned and practiced with incessant care."*
>
> —Johann W. von Goethe

I firmly believe that one should never stop searching for things that can make one wiser and better. Life is not a farce. Life is the greatest gift you will ever receive.

Chapter 2

Diagnosis

The year was 1940, the place St. Louis, Missouri, the location the campus of St. Louis University. In the school gymnasium, packed with guests, I sat on a raised platform along with 109 classmates and a handful of professors. Locked in my hand was a sheepskin proclaiming me an M.D.

I couldn't wait to get out. My head was crammed with knowledge and my heart was ready to burst with great expectations. There were no doubts, no fears; my course was set—or so I thought. Just a few months later, Japan attacked Pearl Harbor, and I found myself trying to dig foxholes on coral beachheads.

Many things have changed since that day in June 1940. Antibiotics were discovered, to cure a long list of disabling and often fatal infections. The word "antibiotic" didn't even exist when I graduated. New and improved vaccines have practically eliminated poliomyelitis, tetanus, diphtheria, and whooping cough. They were killers that today's doctors have never seen. Surgeons routinely repair torn and mangled organs, and if the organs are too far-gone they can perform transplants. The blind are made to see again, the deaf to hear, and the lame to walk.

All these so-called miracles have come to pass since 1940, yet there has not been a corresponding improvement in health. Doctors' offices are full of ailing people. What is wrong?

It has been estimated that 25 to 75 percent of all patient visits to doctors are unnecessary. Many of these individuals present legitimate complaints for which no organic cause can be found. The majority will sooner or later complete exhaustive studies that include blood, urine and tissue analysis, X-ray, CT scans, and MRIs (Magnetic Resonance Imaging). Some are even dumped on psychologists and psychiatrists. Nothing is discovered to explain their pain and discomfort. These are the people who, in the majority are unable, and less frequently unwilling, to face up to the problems and stresses of everyday living. They have been labeled hypochondriacs and much more.

Medical schools have perpetuated and contributed to their growth. Hippocrates, some 400 years B.C., clearly stated that medicine is an art and not a science. Even with the explosion of new technology, his statement rings true today. Recently, a prominent brain researcher lamented, "Even with each brilliant advance in knowledge of the workings of the brain, it only ends up doubling the unanswered questions."

Medical students are carefully drilled to believe that every human action and reaction has a scientific basis in fact. They speak of neurotransmitters and retroviruses, as if the human brain were a computer. The insights of theology and philosophy, and the perception of the artist, are ignored or scorned in the schools. It's remarkable that despite four years of forced feeding on a diet made up exclusively of scientific morsels, we have young doctors who are well versed in the humanities and display a genuine sense of sympathy toward their patients. They should be given a pat on the back.

The media—television, radio, and newspapers—planted the seeds that led to the explosion of hypochondriac-type behavior. My wife and I watch the evening news while we eat dinner. I'm brought up to date on the day's medical advances, and my wife learns what soap to buy. Interspersed with these golden nuggets, we find out who killed whom. How many times have you seen a red-eyed guy, face lined with deep remorse, leaning on his wife? She lovingly says, "It's not your fault, go to Doctor _____, and in two weeks and a couple of follow-up sessions you'll never want to drink again." Then there's this other fellow, who shouts, "I don't have time for pain, give me something that works *fast*!" Instead of the cold product they recommend, I sometimes feel like sending him a prescription for cyanide. It would really be fast—and permanent!

Watching TV you'll discover a place and an expert for any ache or pain you may get or dream up. It doesn't matter if you can't afford it, credit cards and loans are yours for the asking—just call the toll-free number.

In summary, the media scattered the seeds of hypochondria across this land. The medical schools cultivated the ground with the latest diagnostic tools and kept it fertile with pure science. Then, in stepped the lawyers to harvest and claim the crop.

Of course, it's infantile to believe it's all that simple. We've had hypochondria since time immemorial...but think about it.

If you wish to see
The grandeur of the day,
You must blow out
The candle of the idle day.

—Edwin Parker

Chapter 3

Hypochondriasis

What's a hypochondriac?

There are more definitions than Heinz has pickles. The psychologists and psychiatrists are literally splitting hairs to explain and describe it. They've even coined a new word for hypochondriacs: somatics (in Greek, *soma* means "body"). Yet, in the next breath, they inform us that somatics are not really hypochondriacs, and in the process evade answering the original question. Their reasoning goes something like this:

"The somatic somatizes and his somatization indicates a bodily complaint; but there is no disease. The hypochondriac does the same thing, but in addition has a unrealistic fear or false belief of having a disease."

I fail to see the difference and could care less. If a patient discovers blood in his stool and goes to the doctor, that patient is afraid and justifiably worried. When the doctor finds the culprit to be an internal bleeding hemorrhoid, and not cancer, the relief is the same, be the patient a somatic or a hypochondriac. If, in a short space of time, this same patient develops another set or two of symptoms for which the doctor can't find a diagnosis, the person is in jeopardy of being labeled a hypochondriac or somatic.

It's undeniable that there are many people who, in varying degrees, suffer real pain and discomfort brought on by worry, despair, and self-torment. When a known disease isn't found in their distressed bodies, it's no excuse to label them hypochondriac or somatic—both labels are abominations and its time we disposed of them.

At times we all have difficulty dealing with problems and stress. It's unwarranted to point an accusing finger at those who can't solve theirs. Teach—don't judge.

"It is much easier to be critical than to be correct."

—Benjamin Disraeli

Chapter 4

Anatomy

Our bodies are made of microscopic-sized building blocks called cells. In each cell are forty-six ultra-microscopic containers called chromosomes. Locked within each chromosome are miraculous particles known as genes. No one knows how many genes are in a chromosome; it's suspected their number may be staggering. In each gene are coded messages with instructions that determine each cell's destiny. At conception, from a pool of plenty, a single male sperm cell is favored by a single female egg cell. They bind and become one. The consequence is a single fertilized egg cell, containing a total of forty-six chromosomes, twenty-three of which come from "mama" and twenty-three from "papa."

If, by fate, one inherits an extra chromosome from either parent, the individual will be born with "Down's syndrome." Every cell in their body will contain forty-seven chromosomes. The variable but characteristic mongoloid features are a result of the misguided commands issued by a specific gene concealed in this extra chromosome. If one inherits a defective gene, or a gene damaged by pollution, drugs, alcohol, or many yet-undiscovered causes, it's possible to be born with a harelip, spina bifida, or any imaginable deformity.

An example is the children born to mothers who took Thalidomide– a drug promoted as a tranquilizer—during early pregnancy. Some of their children were born without legs or arms. Thalidomide was developed in Europe. Fortunately, it was not approved in the United States, and was sold exclusively in Europe. Otherwise, we might have had an epidemic in the States. The work of a gene does not stop at birth. To keep our "machines" running smoothly, every gene in our bodies stays busy till we die. There is mounting evidence that some neurological diseases, such as Multiple Sclerosis, Parkinson's, Alzheimer's, and Lou Gehrig's disease, are caused by scrambled messages from damaged or diseased genes.

The virus responsible for the flu epidemic circa 1917 has been identified at autopsies in certain cells of patients who died of Parkinson's disease. It is postulated that the virus lay dormant for many years before attacking the gene located in certain brain cells. Some unknown stimulant awakened it to action.

Gregor Mendel opened the door to the genetic secrets that lay hidden in a plant cell. By so doing he showed the world how to grow bigger and better plants. The Russian politicians got so disturbed by his discovery that they forbade their scientists to even consider such a disloyal concept. Genetics was outlawed in the Workers' Paradise. Anyone caught reading such heresy was shipped to Siberia or incarcerated in a mental hospital. Stalin reminded the faithful that Lenin was their god, and no man could control the environment. To date, Russian cell biologists are still working frantically to catch up to our scientists in the field of genetics.

The team of Crick and Watson opened up a whole new field of opportunity, for which they won the Nobel Prize. That field is now named genetic engineering, and its workers molecular or cell biologists. By peering into the gene itself, Crick and Watson were the first to discover the double helix—the very structure of DNA, the genetic material from which will be fashioned an individual human being. That's all we are in this unfathomable universe: specks of genetic matter arranged in a double helix, and seen only through an electron microscope. We know this now, thanks to our Nobel laureates, yet the eternal questions remain: Who made this material and why? Doesn't it make you thirst for knowledge? Does it not make you feel good to have been granted the opportunity to try to answer these questions?

You needn't be learned or famous; anyone with a brain can explore the mysteries of life.

Let me give you an example: Penicillin stared us in the face since the beginning of life. I recall one of our professors in medical school demonstrating how to take a throat culture: "Swab the throat," he said, "with a clean cotton applicator. Carefully open the Petri dish, just enough to streak the culture media with the cotton swab, then cover immediately and incubate for twenty-four hours. If you let too much air in, you'll find the medium covered with mold. You'll never find the bacteria, and you will misdiagnose strep throat." No one asked why air kept the bacteria from growing; we just obeyed and never questioned.

Penicillin kept primitive man from starving: it didn't take long for the aborigine to learn that if he wrapped his meat in leaves or left it on the ground it quickly spoiled, but when by chance he draped it over a tree limb and forgot that he had, he was pleasantly surprised to find it, weeks later, covered with mold, but tasting good. When shopping, you might ask the butcher why the salami is covered with a gray-white mold. He'll probably tell you that it's to keep the meat fresh, but if you persist in questioning him, he may be hard pressed to explain how it got there, where it came from, and how it works.

Dr. Fleming, a British physician, isolated penicillin from a mold and answered the question of where the mold came from, what it's made of, how it works, and, most importantly, how it could be used to cure infectious diseases. Fleming discovered penicillin—it had been on our salami all along!

"We are all continuously faced with a series of opportunities brilliantly disguised as insolvable problems."

—W. P. Prescott, American colonel in the Revolutionary War

"Facts do not cease to exist just because they are ignored."

—Aldous Huxley

"Don't be afraid to take a big step if one is indicated. You can't cross a chasm in two small jumps."

—Lloyd George

Chapter 5

Treatment

We live in a time when it's fashionable to "take care of your body." In the new anatomy, that's from the neck down; the brain is not included.

Does your day begin with turning on the TV, standing in front of the mirror, flapping your limbs and contorting your toes? With unshakable faith you rattle and roll, confident that excavating the fat will resurrect your youthful figure. How long has it been since you opened your eyes with a prayer of thanks, and then planted a seed in the soil of your brain? You'd be surprised how quickly it could sprout into a good deed or idea for the day, and how much better you'd feel.

One evening when I had difficulty going to sleep, I walked downstairs and flipped on the TV; there on the tube was a woman I hadn't seen in fifty years. I recognized her as a former movie star, though time had not been kind to her face. For ten minutes she denounced sugar as an unnatural food that would rot your teeth and transform your kids into hyperactive monsters. How strange: I never knew before that the sugar beets I helped harvest as a kid, and the sugar cane I loved to chew in Puerto Rico, were unnatural and harmful. I had no idea that sugar was a synthetic product manufactured by some greedy corporation that was out to harm us. It's impossible for me to believe that my heart surgeon fed me sugar-water intravenously to injure me after he worked for hours so I could live. Why does my body convert most of the food I eat into sugar to produce energy? Doesn't it know sugar is a poison? It's incredible that no one asked her, "How do you know that?" How I wish I could have asked her whether she still believed the earth was flat. I'm so thankful I wasn't a hyperactive child—I'd never have gotten to enjoy all the candy I ate. (My mother and father owned and ran a sweet shop.)

> *"The greater the ignorance, the greater the dogmatism."*
>
> —Sir William Osler

I believe we are making a real effort to improve our bodies, but when it comes to our brains, we seem to ignore them or try our best to destroy them. Socrates, the Greek philosopher, did his teaching under an olive tree in ancient Athens. His technique was simple and sincere: he taught his young students to think for themselves—to use their brains, and not to assume everything as fact, just because they heard it from their teachers, parents, or government. This so unnerved the teachers and parents that they went straight to their emperor and told him that Socrates was corrupting their children. How dare he have their children question what their elders told them? Though astonished by their assertions, the emperor believed them and, with a sterile mentality, condemned Socrates to death. Socrates drank the prescribed poison—hemlock—and died.

Today, the "authorities" of the media have created for us an illusion of a world in which there is neither hardship nor stress. With a barrage of half-truths, they are attempting to lower our mentality to the level of morons. A perfect world does not exist and never has. We all have problems, and times aren't always pleasant. Experts are of little help, and often create more problems than they solve. The least knowledgeable are usually the most vocal. When it comes to treating ailments brought on by problems and unpleasantness, we have an expert for our every symptom and complaint. Seldom, if ever, do we question their methods.

For the most part, education today consists of conveying information on all subject matter from teacher to student. If by chance a student questions a statement, he is referred to an encyclopedia or the highest authority—the computer. He might not even realize that a computer only regurgitates what another teacher has fed it. The method by which the "factual" statement was established is rarely mentioned. Example: Our learned teacher, the TV, warns us, "Don't feed your child candy or he will become hyperactive." Have you ever asked yourself, "How do they know it's true?" And more importantly, "Through what method was this unenlightened statement arrived at?" Did you ever give thought to the fact that this statement is false?

The Friday-night cocktail party is undoubtedly the best place to find the "experts." The nutrition expert is the easiest to spot: he's the one who attracts the biggest group of neo-intellectuals bearing tankards filled with spirits. No matter how far you back off, you can't help hearing him dogmatically condemning the McDonald's "Big Mac." He makes sure you acknowledge his "expertise," never failing to mention how little our physicians know about nutrition.

I never cease to wonder why it took so long to learn what happened to the "White Castle Hamburger" I loved so much to eat. Why did it take years for my teachers to chart the metabolic pathways this doomed little hamburger had to travel? Why was it digested and crushed by those mean little enzymes scattered throughout the thirty or more feet of tunnel called the intestines? Why was it necessary to sort these particles of meat into protein, carbohydrates, and fat? Why does my body select the proteins to build new cells, and burn the carbohydrates to produce energy to feed itself? If I told you what fat was responsible for, besides making sex possible, you wouldn't believe me.

"Had I lived a natural lifestyle and eaten nothing but organically grown food, I might have spared myself a lot of misery and lived to a grand old age of thirty-five years."
—Bill Bockus, artist and old friend, age eighty-six

"The exact contrary of what is generally believed is often the truth."
—Jean de La Brugere

Chapter 6
Therapists

Difficulty and stress are the winds that propel us on this journey across the unpredictable sea we call life.

Build yourself a good ship with sails that won't rip. You'll find the building material for your ship, and the instructions for sailing, in education. It doesn't need to be formal education; you can teach yourself, through books and free courses, to contemplate history, appreciate art, and understand the basic principles of science. You can learn to enjoy classical music and relax with contemporary or country tunes. You can seek comfort in religion, and stretch the mind in astronomy while pondering life's meaning. Don't procrastinate—make yourself do the things you have to do *now,* not later, whether you like it or not. You'll be pleasantly surprised at how quickly many of your problems will melt away, and how little you'll lean on the opinion of the "experts" you've been programmed to value. You'll be rejuvenated to discover that it makes sense to develop a solid respect for your own common sense and inborn intelligence.

You won't be habitually debilitated by trivia. Head colds, upset stomachs, minor headaches, and backaches won't wipe you out. You won't tremble every time you're compelled to make a decision. You won't be frozen in fear when you're faced with a storm. No matter how rough the sea, you can pilot your ship on a true course when you're equipped, prepared, and confident. When you least expect it, you'll find islands of happiness along your way—relax and enjoy, savor every minute.

Life is tough and often unpleasant. When we are sad and discontented we prefer to communicate it as "not feeling well," and go looking for a healer who will give our undiagnosable illness a label—preferably one that will raise our self-esteem.

There isn't an M.D. worth his salt who can't spot a bunch of symptoms as no disease. His practice will suffer if he tells the patient there's nothing wrong; he must come up with a label. I'm sure you're all familiar with the "Valium scam." The doctor will treat the tired, depressed housewife with understanding and sympathy, then rush her out of the office with a prescription for Valium, a pat on the back, and a statement such as, "Get this prescription filled and I'm sure you'll soon feel better." Some doctors prefer the "vacation scam": they tell you to take a rest, and prescribe a four-week vacation—whether you can afford it or not.

Hypoglycemia was a favorite label for years, especially if the patient came up with two or more of the following symptoms: shakiness, dizziness, sweating, anxiety, fatigue, hunger, headache, or palpitations of the heart. Hypoglycemia can be a serious disease, but it's not that prevalent. Exactly the same symptoms commonly occur in what medically is called functional hypoglycemia, or hypoglycemia brought on by stress and problems. Hypoglycemia means "low blood sugar." In functional hypoglycemia, the symptoms always occur two to three hours after breakfast or lunch, and are promptly relieved by eating. Inexplicably, the patient only complains after dinner; equally mysterious, he can go days without symptoms.

Listening carefully when the patient describes his or her symptoms will usually alert the doctor to the correct diagnosis. If in doubt, he or she can order glucose tolerance tests;

if they're properly interpreted, it's simple to differentiate the real disease from the functional. In the late seventies and early eighties this was a most fashionable disease to have; it was favored by the rich and famous as a means of explaining away their inability to cope with stress and struggle.

The same symptoms ascribed to hypoglycemia are now being used to diagnosis nonexistent "allergies." Patients' blood is tested for all kinds of foods and materials. The results of such tests are not always reliable, and false interpretations and conclusions are common. They're deprived of foods they enjoy, but the patients don't care—they have a label to flaunt.

By no means do I intimate that all healers who use allergy tests to diagnose illness are charlatans. There are a few bad apples in any field. There are a lot of people who are allergic to many foods and other materials; they do get ill and can die if they ignore the fact that they're allergic.

Some time ago, a patient came to me complaining of throbbing headache, dizziness, and palpitations of the heart. I could find no cause for her symptoms so I referred her to an internist. He then sent her to a cardiologist, who in turn sent her to a neurologist, who, in desperation, sent her to an ophthalmologist. The other day I ran into her at the grocery store. With a gleam in her eye and barely perceptible scorn on her face she asked, "Remember me? I'm the one you couldn't cure. I saw five different doctors until Ms. Cray recommended Dr. Braden. He had no trouble finding out what was wrong with me: with just one blood test he was able to tell me that I have "Epstein-Barr Syndrome," and that I've had it for years."

"Are you feeling better?" I asked.

"Oh, yes!" she answered.

"That's nice, I'm happy for you," I concluded as I headed for the cashier stand.

That certainly was a label I hadn't heard used before to explain away a group of symptoms. Strange, I thought the Epstein-Barr virus was the causative agent of mononucleosis.

And only a few days before I had read of a study conducted at a leading university, wherein they found Epstein-Barr antibodies in 90 percent of their students, yet less than 5 percent had ever had mononucleosis. What an opportunity this presents: now people who walk into a healer's office complaining of headache, dizziness, and palpitations of the heart can have their blood drawn, and in 90 percent of them you'll find antibodies for the Epstein-Barr virus. What a beautiful label, "Epstein Barr Syndrome"—your doctor is so scientific, he found the cause of your symptoms; he found the antibodies.

There are healers who will treat any and all mixtures of symptoms with Megavitamins and promise miraculous cures. In his book *Vitamin Politics* (Prometheus Books, 1984), John Fried tells us how the promoters of vitamin quackery were actually helped by politicians to hamper the Food and Drug Administration and other federal agencies in their efforts to protect the public (you and me) against worthless or toxic doses of vitamins. In his introduction, Fried felt that vitamins in massive doses were of no value to 99.9% of the people swallowing them, and that the other 0.1% should be under the care of a qualified physician with expert knowledge of vitamin metabolism problems.

Suffice to say, I heartily agree with Mr. Fried.

The chiropractor is the best known "touch therapist" or healer, and has the largest number of devotees, and I freely admit he has helped people with their symptoms.

In the 1890s, in Iowa, lived a man named Daniel David Palmer. He healed people using a technique known as Mesmerism—a method by which a subject was hypnotized using bright lights, shiny objects, or noises. One day Palmer came upon the idea that nerves carried messages from a higher intelligence that instructed the body to stay well. Since the nerves ran down our backs through a tunnel made up of thirty-three vertebrae and exit through openings in the vertebrae, it made sense to him that if the nerve impulses were blocked, the body would respond with a variety of illnesses. Palmer called this blockage "subluxation" and described it as a vertebra losing its alignment with a vertebra above or below, obstructing the opening and pinching the nerve. By adjusting the vertebra back to its proper place, the patient is cured of his illness.

Palmer's students believed and practiced this method until recently. Now, however, for reasons I don't know, to qualify for a chiropractic degree, the education has been extended to four years instead of the original correspondence course. Palmer would flip in his grave if he knew his followers now study anatomy, bacteriology, physiology, and nutrition. He might say, "How can you be so disloyal to me, the father of the chiropractic method? What hypocrites you are!"

Originally, the osteopath was a touch healer. Andrew Taylor Still was the founder of osteopathy. An M.D., he was a country doctor on the Union side during the Civil War. When his three children died during an epidemic of spinal meningitis he became depressed and disenchanted with the way medicine was then being practiced. Living on a farm, he observed the animals and concluded they took better care of their backs than did man. He began manipulating spines and gave up using medicines to treat the ill. From these beginnings grew the discipline of osteopathy. Among children he was known as the "knuckle-cracking doctor." The osteopathy curriculum too has been extended to include all the subjects taught in medical schools. In California during the 1960s, most of the doctors of osteopathy were incorporated and given M.D. degrees. Today, only a few osteopaths use touch therapy in their practices.

Acupuncture is a type of touch therapy and can be administered by needles, massage, or electric stimulation. It affects its healing and anesthetic properties by releasing energy and allowing it to flow through specified meridians.

Shiatsu is the Japanese version of acupuncture. In the 1950s, Tokijiro Namikosiki popularized this form of treatment in Japan and even got the government to approve its use. The thumb or finger is used to apply pressure over a joint in the body. During treatment, you're supposed to keep your eyes closed and your mouth open. The healer will apply pressure only when you exhale, because that's when your body is softer and looser. They claim Shiatsu is effective in treating diarrhea, asthma, rheumatism, and high blood pressure.

Reiki therapists are led by Ellen Sokolow-Molinari, who took over when Reiki died. Reiki claimed his touch therapy worked on both body and mind simultaneously. He began his healing practice as a disciple of Freud, but wasn't satisfied with psychoanalysis alone and expanded into areas he named "sexeconomy," "political psychology," along with other mind-shaking ideas. He died in 1957 in a Pennsylvania jail, locked up for refusing to appear in court on a charge of transporting "orgone boxes" across state lines. His orgone boxes supposedly contained energy that held healing powers.

Bioenergetics is yet another type of touch therapy. Psychiatrist Alexander Lowen, who had at one time been a student of Reiki's, developed bioenergetics. He didn't believe in the theory of orgone boxes, but embraced Reiki's ideas of attentive healing and psychotherapy. Lowen developed a theory that included psychoanalysis with bodywork. For example, if you complained of a tight jaw or a tight hamstring, he would apply pressure with his fist or finger till it hurt, wanting you to scream with pain until you let out the sadness or rage that caused the muscles to tighten. Lowen didn't hurt you—the pain was already in the muscle, he claimed.

There are other types of touch therapies; I can't discuss all of them. By now I'm sure you recognize that they all have common characteristics: they all assume that an invisible and all-powerful energy flows through our bodies. When this energy is blocked, we become ill. When touch therapy is instituted, the energy gets going again and health and well-being are restored.

I mention these various healers not to deride or condemn their work. I only want to give you insight into what they do and why. It's strictly your decision to seek help when you need it. Where you go is not for me to dictate.

Some ten years ago, I went for acupuncture treatments. My orthopedist recommended I have surgery on my neck. He demonstrated on an X-ray film the arthritic spurs in my neck. These, he said, were compressing the cervical nerves and causing pain whenever I moved my neck to one side or the other. I had a friend who had just returned from China. She was an obstetrician and gynecologist who had retired at age sixty-five and gone to China for two years to study acupuncture. One day soon after her return, we were having lunch in the physicians' dining room at a prominent hospital. Noticing that I winced with pain whenever I turned my head, she asked me why. I told her my problem and confessed my fear of the surgical treatment I was scheduled to have. She said she could help me with acupuncture. "Try it for ten treatments, and if it doesn't help you, then have surgery," she urged.

I made the appointments without hesitation. Two times each week, I would go to her office. The nurse would point me to a room and tell me to remove my shirt, put on a white gown, and recline on a comfortable sofa. Soft music filled the room; it was so mellow that I could have fallen asleep.

In a few minutes, my doctor friend entered. "Good morning, Ed. I'm so glad you came. Please relax. You'll barely feel what I do." She inserted eight acupuncture needles into various areas of my shoulders and upper arms, but not into the neck itself. There was no pain when the needles were inserted. "Stay where you are, Ed, and enjoy the music. I'll be back to remove the needles in ten minutes."

She returned on time and removed the needles. Then she said, "Sit up please and move your head from side to side." I did, and there was much less pain than before. I had only six treatments, because each time the pain was less and less when I turned my head from side to side. After the sixth treatment, I had no pain at all, and it's never returned. Would I ever go back if the pain recurred? Absolutely!

Chapter 7

Solutions

Each of us has bad days. At those times we're difficult to live with. We blame others for how we act. We feel unloved and become unlovable and as a result a nervous cycle is set up. Your husband comes home after a hard day at the office, and instead of asking, "How was your day?" he fails to embrace you and never seeks your comfort. He slams the door and yells, "Why the hell did you plan a big dinner for tonight when you knew that I had to work late?" You interpret his outburst as unprovoked hostility—after all, you too worked all day, fixing a fine dinner. You are hurt, and stand firm against his action, intent on revenge. Soon you're in a verbal battle. Of course, he was wrong, but so were you. Two wrongs have never made a right.

It's hard to close your mouth and change the subject after you've been hurt, yet you must. But it's also very important that you first clearly state your point of contention. Do it and be done with it; don't repeat it over and over. Don't complain the next morning, or repeat your demands of last evening, and by no means keep notes and recite them to him days or weeks later. Instead, try your hardest to say something nice about him. It's not easy, but you can do it. If you keep bringing up the good things your spouse does for you, he or she will turn around in time and complement you in return. Try it again and again—it really works.

We must understand that it's perfectly normal to feel like this, in the same way that it's normal to be physically ill occasionally. It's only the resilience and determination we show in extricating ourselves from our position that will increase our self-esteem and free us from "feeling bad."

For some people, however, the periods of time spent in psychological despair are prolonged. They never seem to get over their sense of hurt. Like children who keep taking the scabs off their wounds, they never let the sores heal. They seem to enjoy the hurt. Try as they might, such people appear to be unable to deal with problems. They seem hemmed in, surrounded by the high walls of their difficulties. All they want to do is get revenge for their pain, no matter what.

Just as the drunk must admit he's a drunk and want to quit before he can stay sober, so the people who can't handle problems must admit that they lack self-respect before they can get rid of the illness brought on by their fragility.

It's not easy to convince people suffering from troubles that they alone are responsible for their problems: it disturbs them profoundly; it removes all their excuses.

If you are a husband, wife, or true friend, it's your job to motivate your loved one to improve his or her own lot. Motivation itself is the most difficult seed to implant. You must create situations in which people can look at their lives with satisfaction and admiration, and help them feel that they are really worthwhile. If occasions arise when you must criticize, be sure your criticism is constructive and never destructive. Take every opportunity to praise. Encourage the person to create: for example, to plant a garden, learn to paint, take music lessons, exercise, play golf or tennis, or swim, take long walks, or learn to recognize birds and plants.

If you're the one who's troubled, instead of feeling sorry for yourself, do something active and enjoyable. Don't limit yourself to reading books in your free time; get on a path of extroversion rather than introversion. Act rather than contemplate.

Most people who aren't feeling well because of nervous tension and other difficulties firmly believe they would be happy if only their spouse weren't crabby, weren't an alcoholic, or didn't lie or cheat. This is a mistaken judgment. No one has a natural right to happiness; it is obtained only through hardship and great effort. The very troubles that we hate so much—the crabbing, cheating, lying, and drinking—are instrumental in attaining happiness. It's these we must overcome, and in doing so gain respect and contentedness.

Talk therapists, touch practitioners, and physicians who attempt to cure miseries resulting from troubles and anxiety offer no sound solutions. Despite the purest of motives, they actually harm you by encouraging dependency. It is vital to avoid misconceptions about the nature of life, and expose as fallacy the idea that because we're unhappy and ineffective we need "expert" intervention. We alone are responsible for our predicament. We are not slaves to our environment or to our brain biochemistry. We are free, and with kindred support we can change ourselves for the better. With the right help—from our true friends and loved ones—we can arrive at happiness.

I believe "Be good and goodness will find you. Get mad and madness will envelope you."

The following is one of my favorite poems, because it is filled with thought and enduring worth.

Rugby Chapel

Most men eddy about
Here and there—eat and drink,
Chatter and love and hate,
Gather and squander, are raised
Aloft, are hurl'd in the dust
Striving blindly, achieving
Nothing; and then they die—
Perish; and no one asks
Who or what they have been,
More than he asks what waves,
In the moonlit solitudes mild
Of the midmost Ocean, have swell'd,
Foam'd for a moment, and gone.

—Mathew Arnold, British poet of the 1800s

The Irish are much noted for their love of alcohol. I have heard many times that if you walk along the streets of Ireland, every fourth shop is a pub. I've never been in Ireland, so I can't say it's true. Nonetheless, it reminds me of an old joke.

A first-grade teacher in Ireland had a husband who never failed to imbibe at the least provocation. She believed that it was her duty to impress on her students the extreme dangers of alcohol, so she dug up some worms at home one day, put them in a jar, and brought them to her class. "Students," she said, "I will demonstrate why you should not drink alcohol." She placed two glasses on the desk where all could see. Into one she poured water, and into the other, alcohol. Into both she put some worms. "Look closely now," she said. After a few minutes she pulled the worms from the glass that held water, and they all wiggled, lively, on her desk. "Now watch," she exclaimed as she picked the worms out of the glass filled with alcohol. All the worms were stiff and dead. While doing all this, she noticed a boy near the end of the room who was fidgeting constantly and paying little attention. At the end of the demonstration, she shouted, "Johnny, did you understand what I was doing?"

"Yes, teacher," he answered.

"Then tell me what you learned."

"I learned that if you drink alcohol you'll never get worms," he answered.

There is a lesson for all of us in this tale. Johnny, like all his cohorts, heard the same talk and saw the same results, but his interpretation was contrary to the teacher's intent. This was due solely to his careless concentration. At times, we are all guilty of the same. We should never forget to exercise prudence in responding to information.

Section Three

Chapter 1

Marijuana

The three most dangerous drugs that have the capacity to enslave people beyond any power are:

1. *Marijuana, and its most potent form, hashish.*
2. *Cocaine, and its most popular form, crack.*
3. *Opium, from which codeine, morphine, and heroin are made.*

All three are vegetable products; their active ingredients occur naturally in plants. However, great skill is needed to cultivate the plants and recover the active substances.

Lets start with marijuana, a narcotic made from the leaves and flowers of the hemp plant. The stalks are not thrown away but are treasured for their tough and enduring fibers. When prehistoric man first saw the hemp plant, with its pretty leaves and flowering tops, he yanked the plant out of the ground and took the bouquet to his mate, who was pleased. They both handled the leaves and flowers; soon their hands smelled good, but their fingers were getting very sticky, so they licked them clean—they were tasty and minty. They soon found that smelling and licking the leaves and flowers was great fun; they laughed and laughed—they got "high!" It didn't take them long to discover that the stems and stalks were composed of tough bast fibers, so she used them to weave her baskets, and he found that the stalks made good rope that helped him build sturdy, long-lasting shelters.

Centuries later, man learned to hollow fallen logs, and for the first time was able to travel on water. At first he used large sticks to make these hollowed logs move through the water, but he soon learned to increase its speed and range with a sail—yes, the sails were made from hemp fibers—and he began to discover other lands and people.

It became easy to exchange the precious "happy-making" hemp plant for foods he hadn't seen before; thus trade and drug trafficking was born. Today the United States government grows hemp plants in the southern states, but only for cordage; the resin is destroyed.

In a Chinese book of medicine dated 2737 B.C., the Emperor Shaw Nung warned that the hemp plant was not the way to paradise, but instead lined the road to hell. He ordered his people to destroy all the hemp plants in China, and executed those who didn't comply.

Full-grown hemp plants produce a resin that concentrates in the top leaves and flowers. The resin contains over eighty active chemicals. The most psychoactive (mind altering) is THC (tetrahydrocannabinol).

Marijuana is known by names such as pot, grass, and reefer, and in its purest form, hashish. A lot of the marijuana sold on our streets comes from Mexico. It's the cheapest. The Mexicans chop up the whole plant, leaves, stalks, flowers, and roots. It contains about 0.5 percent THC. Occasionally, it is surreptitiously adulterated with LSD or PCP to give it more bang. From Columbia, more of the leaves and flowers are used and less of the stalks. It contains 1–2 percent THC. Marijuana that comes from Thailand, Hawaii, and California is made mostly from the top leaves and flowers of carefully cultivated plants that have a higher quality and quantity of resin. Called *sinsemilla,* meaning "seedless," it contains up to 60 percent THC, and is potent, expensive, and in great demand.

Hashish is the purest form of marijuana, and comes mainly from Asia. It is made almost entirely of resin from cultivated and selected hemp plants. Hashish, which means "assassin" or "murderer," was fed to soldiers in Asia and Europe to make them fearless and senseless in battle.

During the conquest of Mexico, the Spanish observed the natives smoking marijuana and, because of its effects, forbade their own soldiers to use it.

The marijuana sold on our streets is getting more potent each year. More and more of it is grown in California. The plants are carefully selected and cultivated, producing purer, more potent, and abundant resin. A professor at the University of California at Davis stated, "If as much energy and time were devoted to growing tomatoes as is used to make stronger marijuana, we would be growing ninety-pound tomatoes today."

Marijuana is the "master" key to slavery. When you start using pot, you get it free from a school chum. You're not a seller or a junkie, but you're soon smoking it several times a week. Now you begin sharing the free samples with your friends. You buy an ounce, sell some, and keep the free pot for yourself. Sooner or later you buy a full pound. The guy you're buying it from sells other drugs also. Now you're familiar with opiates, cocaine, crystal meth, LSD, and PCP, etc., and you're involved in the drug culture. Ninety percent of hard-core addicts will tell you they started in this way. I have worked in free clinics for the past thirty years, so believe me, that figure is correct.

Marijuana is especially harmful to children and adolescents, because it stops them from maturing emotionally. When they're "loaded," they'll laugh at seeing their own parents in pain. They suffer permanent impairment in short-term memory and learning abilities; kids on pot just aren't with it in school. You can spot kids on pot—they're turned on and tuned out; they're scrambled, "high," and don't care. Pot can also harm the body's immune system and cause hormonal damage.

An eight-year old was told that pot and alcohol were safe—and believed it. "I kept telling myself it was safe, but after a while I just didn't care anymore," she said. "I was getting loaded on anything I could get my hands on—PCP, LSD, crystal meth, crack." One year later she was found in bed, dead of an overdose. Whether it was accidental or deliberate will never be known. Unfortunately, we have no sure cure for drug addition; the only weapon we have is prevention.

The most remarkable aspect of substance abuse, be it pot, crack, or heroin, is the biological process of dependence. We don't know how it happens or how to stop it; we don't even know why some people become addicted to pot after just a few days' use and others take much longer. One thing, however, is certain: all users eventually get addicted.

A chronic pot smoker will never admit he's unable to stop using it—he defends his use by saying he is unwilling to stop.

THC is soluble in fat, but won't dissolve in water. The brain and our sex glands contain a lot of fat. When we use marijuana, it's stored for days, perhaps weeks, in all the parts of our bodies where there's fat. This is why, unlike alcohol, we don't get hangovers from using pot to get high.

Pot makes you feel good because it acts on the brain, which, once it is repeatedly stimulated to intoxication, will never forget the pleasurable experience. A definite biological change takes place in the brain, which produces a substance or process, not fully identified as yet, that brings on an irresistible urge to use pot again. This urge to use pot is so strong that the tendency to relapse persists for many years, if not a lifetime.

Pot today is ten times stronger than it was in the seventies. Many young and old people are now using marijuana on a daily basis. What happens to them?

1. *They lose their ability for new learning—we can prove this with psychological testing.*

2. *They develop difficulty in tracking lights, especially at night, which puts them and us at risk when they drive under the influence of pot.*
3. *Some get unexplained nosebleeds.*
4. *Others complain of sore throats that don't culture out any organisms.*
5. *They can develop persistent coughs and wheezing despite no previous history of asthma or even any family history of asthma. They do not respond to bronchodilators, antihistamines, or cortisone. The chronic pot smoker has damaged his bronchial tubes, and no antibiotic will cure him.*
6. *Some will switch to cocaine or opiates when marijuana no longer satisfies their needs.*
7. *Some will eventually mature and stop using pot of their own free will.*

We cannot allow our children to experiment with anything so dangerous as pot. It should never be legalized. Many a child and adolescent thinks he is buying pleasure, when in reality he is selling himself as a slave.

Chapter 2

Cocaine

Along the Amazon River, near the jungle's edge grows a coca shrub whose leaf contains an irresistible power. Chew it and in a few minutes you're transformed from a troubled, insecure, worrisome nobody into an individual of authority, in full control and with influence over others—or so it seems to you!

Hidden in the leaf is a substance of extraordinary powder called cocaine. In its pure form, cocaine is a bitter crystal with the chemical formula of $C_{17}H_{21}NO_4$. It is often referred to as white gold. Ounce for ounce, in today's underground market, it's four to ten times more valuable than gold itself.

All the cocaine in the world is grown on the Eastern slopes of the Andes in Columbia, Peru, and Bolivia, where it is processed, and then smuggled into the United States and Europe. I have heard, but have no proof, that attempts are being made to grow the coca shrub in the United States, somewhere in the mountains of New Mexico. The coca shrub grows wild in South America, where the natives have chewed its leaves for thousands of years. In the sixteenth century, the Spaniards, during their conquest of the region, observed but did nothing to stop this habit. They felt it made the natives more willing to work and easier to subdue, so they left well enough alone.

The same is true today: the ruling classes don't dare interfere with the native use of coca leaves. The leaf plays a major role in those nations' lives: it's part of their customs, culture, and religion. Trying to stop it would bring on widespread revolt.

In the twentieth century, explosive advances in agriculture and chemistry changed things to what they are now. Farmers are encouraged to grow coca plants instead of vegetables. If they fail to obey, their crops are destroyed by herbicides by order of organized crime families. To keep from starving, they obey; small farms are especially vulnerable to such coercion.

The natives are taught to dig pits, line them with plastic, and fill them with mature coca leaves. Then they're shown how to incorporate kerosene, sulfuric acid, sodium bicarbonate, and other chemicals, to turn the whole mess into cocaine paste. To keep the law from interfering, and the pilots from finding these pits, they're instructed to dig them in the jungle. Some farms are even booby-trapped with mines to keep the police away. Next they must find runners to take the coca paste to a factory that refines the paste into pure cocaine. These runners are usually kids or young mothers.

In Peru two young mothers, aged eighteen and twenty-five, were arrested carrying coca paste. They knew nothing of the drug problem; they needed money to feed their children and themselves, and were paid to transport. The eighteen-year-old had no husband and was pregnant. She got seventy-five dollars to carry the paste by bus from the farm to the factory. The older woman knew the consequences, but her husband had left her, and she had five kids to feed. Both women got ten years in prison. Peruvian prisons are full of natives who really didn't realize that carrying the paste was an offense. They stay ten years in jail, where mothers are separated from their children.

Others who don't get caught may smoke the paste and soon become addicted. Drug dealers put coca paste in regular cigarettes and give them to youngsters free, so when they get hooked they have to become carriers to get money to pay for their daily dose of coca paste. Some addicts smoke eighty to 100 cigarettes laced with coco paste every day. By smoking paste, they also consume the kerosene, sulfuric acid, and other chemicals that are still in the paste, because it hasn't yet gone to the refinery to remove them. The result is not only damage from smoking, but also brain damage from the toxic chemicals.

The following confession is from a boy, once a college student, now a lost soul:

"I don't even remember my age—I think I was born in January. Once people see you like this, you can't get work. This life unfortunately is easy to enter, but it's hard to get out. At first I smoked marijuana and liked it very much, then I tried coca paste. I was scared because I had heard it's bad, but I kept using it many times. I know that it kills you little by little, but I can't help using it. I gotta get out of this garbage. I used it for twelve years. I'm trying- I'm trying to stop, but I can't. I know it kills."

Working in the clinics, I've heard this litany over and over. These are desperate people, and very few get rid of the addiction, even with treatment.

In Peru, parents in despair are turning to radical treatments and experimental surgery. One psychologist there uses massive doses of tranquilizers to reduce addicts to a near infantile state, and then tries to restructure their attitudes for months at a time, while depriving them of the coca paste. It doesn't work.

In another clinic, in Lima, Peru, they refer these incorrigible victims to a hospital for brain surgery—a most controversial brain operation called a singulotomy. A sixteen-year-old said, "Paste is the worst rubbish, the worst thing in the world." This boy was the twenty-ninth patient to have a singulotomy in Peru. He and his family chose it as a last resort. He was scared stiff of having the operation, but he was more afraid of the addiction that had killed his older brother a year earlier, so he agreed to it. In this surgery, a part of the brain is removed from deep inside the brain itself—the area that provides us our senses of pleasure and that satisfies our hunger, thirst, and sex drive. When you take cocaine, it goes directly to the same area and induces a fierce craving. The theory is that by removing a part of the singulum, which contains transmission lines between the brain's centers of pleasure and conscious behavior, you remove the craving.

Few operations in the world evoke such vehement argument. We ask, "Might this five-hour radical operation eliminate life's other pleasurable sensations? Are we witnessing human progress, or recklessness?" Right or wrong, this operation is an undeniable testament to the power of cocaine.

This lad was able to leave the hospital after a few weeks and seemed fairly normal. However, in one year, half of the twenty-nine operated patients had relapsed into cocaine addiction—one of them this sixteen-year-old.

Authorities would like to convince you that progress is being made to eliminate addiction. Don't you believe it. Almost every day you can read in the newspaper, hear on the radio, or see on TV that huge amounts, sometimes in the tons and worth many millions of dollars are seized by the police and incinerated. This seizure is good, but hardly enough. It represents at most 10 percent of the total amount produced. Each year production expands markedly.

Peru and other South American countries want helicopters, planes, and arms to fight the drug traffic; some want armies, but the area is too large to police, and probably nothing will stop production. More importantly, the profits are so unimaginably enormous that the mafia and the corrupt drug lords will never allow anyone to stop it.

One day in the eighties, the president of Peru addressed the United States from the presidential palace, in Lima. He said, "There are many things for which we are very grateful: literature, art, technology, medicine, many things, but we certainly are not grateful for sending weapons and money to fight the production of cocaine. I believe this drug problem is much more a problem of the United States and other consuming countries than it is of the producing countries. Stop using cocaine and all of the South American countries will stop producing it! With no demand, there results no production."

Those who use cocaine seek a euphoric sense of success and power, but instead find themselves in oblivion. Man has survived the ages using a different source of magic, ultimately greater than any other: it is the power to understand, to overcome; it is a hope of the hopeless, it is the human mind. Use it!

> *"Out of intense complications, intense simplifications emerge."*
>
> —Winston S. Churchill

Chapter 3

Crack

Crack is cocaine, and nothing but cocaine. The sleazy dealers peddling dope call it crack; the addicts know it as "rock." It's a form of cocaine, and by a simple process using baking soda, is easily made to look like rock candy.

When crack is smoked, it's rapidly absorbed through the lungs, and a high concentration in the bloodstream is quickly achieved and delivered to the brain. A single hit of crack produces an intense, wrenching rush in a matter of seconds. "It feels like the top of your head is going to blow off," some addicts say. There is an instant, though short-lived, euphoria—a "two-minute high." But other effects take place just as quickly: in minutes the flash high is followed by a crashing low that leaves a user craving another hit. The user risks life-threatening convulsions, temperatures can go to 115° F, blood pressure rises alarmingly, and brain hemorrhages (strokes) can occur that can cripple or kill. Many have died from heart attacks due to the intense spasming of the coronary arteries, and the older the user, the greater the risk.

The drug dealer will never mention the risks; he'll only brag about how good and cheap it is. Most small-time drug peddlers are themselves addicts. They must sell to buy food to live, and drugs to quell their unremitting cravings, so they push you to buy.

To sustain the "high" the user must refill his water-filled pipe with crack every twenty minutes or so. It doesn't take a mathematician to figure out that it's going to cost you a lot more than if you snorted street cocaine.

Another way to get a quick "high" is by "free-basing" the powdered cocaine with ether. You can smoke the end product, but you take a great risk to make it. Ether is an extremely volatile, flammable liquid, which makes it extremely dangerous to use. We all learned that in 1980, when the talented comedian Richard Pryor set himself on fire while "free-basing" at home. He suffered extreme pain for a very long time, and very nearly died.

I've had more than one coke addict try to argue with me that crack is not cocaine, because, "its much better and quicker." They won't accept the fact that it's just another form of the same destructive animal.

In 1884, Sigmund Freud became interested in cocaine. He and his colleague, Karl Koller, got in a legal fight as to who first discovered its use as a local anesthetic. Koller won in court. Freud called attention to cocaine's pleasant effect on mood, and its ability to reduce fatigue. As a result cocaine was incorporated into a number of tonics and patent medicines.

"Vin Moriaini" was a wine that contained cocaine. So successful was this wine that its originator, Angelo Mariconi, had testimonials from popes, monarchs and American presidents. Even Jules Verne and Thomas Edison mentioned how great a wine it was. Coca-Cola originally spiked its beverage with cocaine, but eliminated it in 1903 after many complaints.

Throughout history, the major means of administration was oral ingestion. Cocaine went into disrepute, and by 1914 only a small segment of the population used it. It wasn't until the 1960s that there was a major resurgence of its popularity. It was hailed as the "champagne of drugs." It became fashionable to snort cocaine—even golden spoons were used for sniffing it at parties. It didn't take long before "free-basing," smoking, and intravenous use were discovered.

Chapter 4
Opium

In Greece and Asia grows a deceptive plant, usually less than four feet tall, sprouting lovely flowers. Embraced by its petals is a seed-packed pod. As soon as the petals fall, and the pod becomes denuded, workers are summoned. The green seed capsule is slit, and a milky juice oozes out, which is allowed to dry until it turns brown and gummy. This sticky substance is rolled into balls and taken to workshops where it's refined into opium, the world's most powerful narcotic.

Some addicts eat this pure opium or smoke it in pipes; others inject it with hypodermic needles or inhale it like snuff. It's not used in medicine as such, but, physicians use compounds made from opium, namely morphine and codeine. Morphine is the most effective painkiller a doctor can give you. Heroin is more effective, however, because it's three times as potent as morphine, the government has banned its manufacture and use in the United States. I can't write a prescription for it—but you can buy it on the streets.

Heroin was made by the Germans in the late 1800s and touted as the drug to cure morphine addiction. Our government actually sanctioned its use, and in 1898 declared that heroin was non-addictive—you could buy it without a prescription. By 1914, one in every 400 Americans was a narcotic addict, most of them housewives. You could send your kid to the drugstore to buy Miss Winslow's Soothing Syrup, $1.74 for an eight-ounce bottle. It contained 40 percent alcohol plus opium. What happened? By four o'clock in the afternoon, a homemaker had no more backache, and after a few more swigs, no more hot flashes—and by midnight the kids were screaming for supper.

My maternal grandmother was one of those addicts. She got her "asthma medicine" by mail from a firm in Kansas City,

Missouri, and became furious if the mail was late. Her rage frightened me. I didn't know why then, but I do now—the "asthma medicine" was laced with opium.

Opium and its derivatives, morphine and codeine, give the user the illusion that he has mastery over situations about which he can do little or nothing. Coupled with the power these drugs have to give intense physical and emotional pleasure, the user is unable to resist taking the drug again and again.

Heroin is produced by heating morphine with acetic acid, thus tripling its strength. In the body, heroin rapidly breaks down into morphine, so its pharmacological action is the same.

In 1832 the French produced codeine from opium and heralded it to the world: "Take codeine—it will abolish the opium habit."

"Humbug," I say. I asked a talented singer once why she kept injecting heroin into her veins. "It makes me feel that I just put on a very expensive mink coat and I'm ready to go," she answered. An eighteen-year-old, gifted with a golden voice, she was found dead in her bed two months later. The autopsy revealed the cause of death: "Respiratory failure from an overdose of opium."

It has been reported in the media that in New York City, 1 percent of all adults who die each year do so from opium overdoses. Lots of street opium and heroin contains little or no opium, so when the user gets the "real stuff," he or she accidentally overdoses. I'm sure that young singer died this way.

Opium has been used since long before Christ was born. The Sumerians used clay tablets to record their use of opium; it's mentioned forty-two times—and that was more than 5,000 years ago. These people lived in the lower part of Mesopotamia (now Iraq). They built great temples and palaces; they were skilled craftsmen and artisans; they made spears, armor, and chariots for their armies; they probably invented writing. This was a most distinguished civilization. Their clay tablets show all, for us to learn: Use opium and you become a slave.

Today we still have no cure for opium addiction. For over thirty years we've dispensed methadone through licensed clinics that are subjected to federal, state, and local regulation. Methadone is a potent drug, which affects the user's lifestyle and outlook profoundly. It's not a cure; it's only a means of enabling the rest of us to feel that we're doing something.

Chapter 5

Crank

In the 1930s, our chemists produced amphetamine, which was first sold in the form of inhalers for head colds and asthma. Soon, however, it became widely known for producing feelings of well-being and elation, and causing loss of weight, so it was made available in pill form.

In the 1940s, epidemics of amphetamine abuse occurred in several countries in Europe and Asia. By the 1950s it became the most popular weight-reduction drug in the United States, and the drug most frequently abused by truck drivers, athletes, night-shift workers, and students. Late in the fifties, federal controls were enacted to regulate its manufacture, but they were ineffective.

Two of the most frequently prescribed amphetamines for weight reduction were Dexedrine and Desoxyn. Ask your parents—I'm sure they'll recognize the names. Finally, in 1970, Congress passed The Controlled Substance Act, which strongly regulated the manufacture of amphetamines, but today the government still allows drug companies to manufacture Dexedrine, Desoxyn, and other amphetamines. It also warns physicians to prescribe amphetamines only if indicated—and never for pleasure.

Obviously this act and warning have been grossly ignored. Since then many analogs of amphetamines have been manufactured, of which the most widely known and used is methamphetamine, known on the streets as "crank." The smokeable form of methamphetamine, called "Joe," is the most prized by addicts. Just like crack cocaine, it brings on euphoria in seconds, and lasts many times longer than cocaine—it's the poor man's crack.

You can even make it in your own backyard from readily available chemicals and recipes. Sure, you can be blown up in the process, but who cares? For 200 bucks' worth of cookware and less than a thousand dollars' worth of chemicals, you can cook out enough methamphetamine to sell for thousands of dollars. Money, lots of money, is all that counts.

At first, illegal use of methamphetamine got wildly popular when it became available in capsule form, and was known as "speed." Today, it's usually produced as a crystalline white powder that's either sniffed through the nose or mixed with water and injected intravenously. Many addicts fear needles, and also know that they can contract AIDS and other infectious diseases if they use a needle used earlier by someone who has such a disease. So, smoking has become their method of choice. Any drug that can be smoked gets into the brain in much higher concentration and in only seconds, whereas, if swallowed or sniffed, takes ten to thirty minutes to act.

Methamphetamine can bring on chest pain, palpitations, and shortness of breath. Blood pressure rises, the heart races, and body temperature rises. In some users, it can induce such symptoms as agitation, anxiety, hallucinations, delirium, and convulsions—and even death.

In conclusion, methamphetamine (crank) is a powerful and dangerous drug, especially since, as a "street drug," it's often mixed with cocaine, LSD, and other hazardous drugs. You really don't know what the devil you're taking.

"Ecstasy" is just another analogue of methamphetamine: chemically, it's 3, 4-Methylenedioxy-N-Methylamphetamine (MDMA), which has been popular for over twenty years. It can shoot your temperature to over 107° F in a hurry. It causes the same symptoms as methamphetamine. It too can kill—and has.

There are many other drugs that wreak havoc in the brain, but I'll only mention a few.

PCP or "angel dust," as it is called on the streets, is made of cyanide and benzene. Drug firms once manufactured it as veterinary medicine, but no longer—now it's made illegally in secluded homes and garages for the drug user hell-bent on thrills. When consumed, it makes the user see objects as melting or moving in wave-like fashion. Sensory impressions become overwhelming; users go into a state where colors are "heard" and sound is "seen." Time seems to pass very slowly, boundaries appear to disintegrate, and the user may feel a sense of oneness with the universe. Thoughts begin to assume extraordinary significance. However, users often experience rapid mood swings, from gaiety to depression, and from elation to terror, and vice versa.

"Bad trips" are common. Images can be unpleasant, and panic reactions occur, accompanied by intense anxiety and fear, leading to completely psychotic states that may last forty-eight hours. PCP is the only drug we know that, with just a single exposure, can derange the chemistry of the brain, the effects of which can last for years. LSD, another hallucinogen, was synthesized from ergot in 1938. Its hallucinatory effects are much the same. It too can produce "bad trips."

Mescaline, made from mescal, a small cactus, has its advocates. It's just as powerful as LSD. LSD and mescaline were used in psychotherapy and for research on mental illness. Both mimic the symptoms of schizophrenia. Eating peyote and certain Mexican mushrooms can also cause similar symptoms, but these are usually much milder.

Worldwide, many other drugs lie hidden in plants that grow wild and remain undiscovered. You can be assured chemists will break down their formulas, and build analogues *ad infinitum,* soon after they are found.

The public has adopted DuPont Chemical Company's motto, "Better living through chemistry." For good or ill, win or lose, it's the game we all play, whether we want to or not. We, the public, have adopted it as the gospel of today.

On a dare, a thirteen-year-old boy—an "A" student, with no apparent problems—injected PCP intravenously. He was hospitalized with delusions, thinking that people were taking away his soul. Eight years later, he blew his head off with a gun. On autopsy no drugs were found; as far as could be determined, he'd never used illegal drugs, except for that one time at age thirteen.

A doctor friend of mine told me, "On her way home from work, my secretary stopped at a bar and ordered a drink, drank some of it, then went to the bathroom, and came back to finish her drink. In less than ten minutes she started screaming that the bartender and the people around her were plotting to kill her. She was driven home, where her mother tried to comfort her, and was briefly successful, but minutes later, the woman tried to strangle her mother, believing that the mother was trying to kill her in a religious sacrifice ritual. She had to be taken by ambulance to the hospital. A "friend" later admitted having put LSD in her drink while she was in the bathroom—"to have some fun," he said.

One should never leave a drink unattended in a public place!

One Saturday afternoon while vacationing with my family in Laguna Beach, California, a friend of mine called and asked if I'd help him in the emergency room. "I'm overwhelmed with patients and exhausted from work and lack of sleep," he pleaded. I promptly went and pitched in. Around midnight, while my friend the doctor lay sleeping on a cot, an ambulance roared in and delivered a young girl, who lay there crying, "I can't move my arms and legs. Oh, God, help me, help me!" It was obvious she had broken her neck and severed her spinal cord. The neurosurgeon was called immediately and arrived promptly.

"Quadriplegic. I'll take her to surgery at once, but there's little hope that I can help." We found out later that she had taken LSD and, in a state of euphoria, had shouted, "I can walk on air." She was on the roof of a five-story Laguna Beach hotel at the time; she couldn't walk on air.

Chapter 6

Prescription Drugs

Oh, how I wish and pray I could write a prescription to stop the use of illegal drugs! The "magic bullet" doesn't exist; maybe it will, someday, but today there's no magic solution to the problem of drug abuse.

By now you'll have noticed that I've made no reference to socially accepted and legal drugs, such as alcohol and nicotine. They're equally dangerous, and much too important to deal with briefly here. I hope to make them the subject of a later treatise; sedatives and tranquilizers need discussion too, and I'll address them then, time permitting.

Nearly every day, I read, see, or hear about a "junkie." They can be doctors, lawyers, chaplains, artists, writers, super-educated individuals, or plain ignorant beings. No matter their status, a junkie is still a junkie, and none is immune to the horrific effects of using illegal drugs, or "junk" as I prefer to call them. When they run out of junk, they'll sell their souls, their lovers' souls, or anything valuable they can get their hands on—when they need "the fix," come hell or high water, they'll do anything to get it, and screw the consequences!

I've read and heard a lot of baloney about legalizing junk drugs to stop the myriad crimes that are drug related. You'd have to be brainless to believe this nonsense. No evil is ever stopped by making it legal.

Edwin Parker, M.D.

Drug use and abuse are killers. Marijuana, cocaine, and opium are killers, and they're not alone: our chemists are wizards at producing "designer drugs." One of the most popular and most deadly is fentanyl, known on the streets as "China white" or "Persian white." Dealers often sell fentanyl as heroin. The supply is easier to get than heroin. Because of its potency, fentanyl has killed many. In its most powerful form, fentanyl is administered during surgery by an anesthesiologist (the doctor who puts you to sleep before you're operated on). It's the preferred anesthetic for heart surgery. It's well known that most physicians who commit suicide choose fentanyl as their killer—it's deadly, quick, and final.

Clandestine chemists bang out new synthetic compounds faster than you can imagine. So far, over 200 variations—called analogues—of fentanyl have been produced.

The indisputable fact is, when you buy on the street, only God knows what other crap you're getting in the junk you purchase. For example, LSD is sometimes secretly added, to give the buyer a bigger kick. Heroin is sometimes mixed with cocaine or crystal meth to give them more punch. Street dealers often dilute the junk they sell with baking powder, sugar, or even arsenic, to increase the amount they have to sell. Most, if not all, street drugs, including crack, crank, crystal meth, ecstasy, LSD, and PCP are made by clandestine chemists in surreptitious laboratories. These labs are filthy, and unbelievably sleazy—they're land mines ready to be exploded by just a spark, because of the ether used in making the junk. Many labs have blown up, killing the makers, who care little about control, or whether the people they sell to live or die.

Money is all that counts; the bounty is mind-blowing. Who would be dumb enough to swallow, inhale, or inject this junk? I'm unable to answer the question. Perhaps William James could, if he were alive today. He wrote,

"Sow an act and you reap a habit, sow a habit and you reap a characteristic, sow a characteristic and you reap a destiny."

As a professor at Harvard University of Psychology, he stressed the importance of setting a goal, for which discipline and reading are needed at first, and cultivating the right good habits, which carry you in the direction you want to go. With constant repetition, the action becomes habitual and self-sustaining, practically automatic, as are the benefits.

Ernest Hemingway made it a habit to write at least 450 words every day, whether he wanted to or not. Franz Liszt practiced scales and exercises daily; this made him one of the greatest pianists.

Voltaire said, "Cultivate your garden, good habits deserve special attention." Henry David Thoreau said, "The cost of a thing is the amount of what I will call 'Life' which is required to be exchanged for it, immediately or in the long run."

The drug habit is the most difficult to break. I'm certain any of you could recite many a sad true story. I know I could write pages of examples, but I won't; instead, I'll tell you about the life of the surgeon William S. Halsted, M.D., a story that covers most bases.

On September 23, 1852 in New York City, William Stuart Halsted was born, the son of William Mills Halsted, president of Halsted, Harris and Company, a textile-importing firm. His mother was Mary Louise Haines.

The Halsteds were a wealthy family who occupied a prominent position financially and philanthropically. William's early education was at Andover, a private school. It was a burden to him. In 1870 he entered Yale University with no goal in mind. His grades were poor, but he distinguished himself in athletics. He was captain of the Yale football team. He admits that in his senior year, because of boredom and without any other reason, he purchased two textbooks on the spur of the moment: *Gray's Anatomy of the Human Body,* and John C. Dalton's *Physiology.*

Reading them simply out of curiosity at first, Halsted conceived an overwhelming interest in medicine; he knew then that he had to become a physician—his goal was set. When he graduated from Yale in 1874, he immediately enrolled and began medical studies at the College of Physicians and Surgeons in New York City.

There he became a student assistant to Professor of Physiology John C. Dalton, the author of the textbook that had led him to a medical career. He graduated among the top ten of his class in 1877, which won him a most coveted position as an intern at Bellevue Hospital.

After finishing his internship in the fall of 1878, Halsted went to Europe for two years. He studied in Austria, Germany, and Vienna, chiefly in basic sciences and surgery, and particularly in anatomy. He was profoundly determined to become the best surgeon possible, and Europe was the only place to get this specialized training.

In 1880 he returned to New York, where he proved his worth in record time. The College of Physicians and Surgeons in New York City appointed him to the faculty. He was their pride and joy—he got his M.D. there.

In just a few months he became chief of surgery at the highly ranked Roosevelt Hospital. He also served as a surgical consultant to five other top-rated hospitals in the New York area, including Bellevue. It was a period of arduous work: he spent mornings operating at Roosevelt Hospital, and afternoons and evenings at the other hospitals, as he was needed—and still found the time to teach at the school from which he graduated.

In 1881 Halsted achieved what was probably the first successful blood transfusion in the United States. He intervened at one of the hospitals where his sister was dying from a postpartum hemorrhage. "After checking the hemorrhage," he said, "I transfused my sister by drawing into a syringe, from one of my veins, and injected it immediately into hers." His sister survived. Just two years later his mother fell dangerously ill from an infected gall bladder full of stones. He operated and saved her life.

By 1884, Halsted was at the height of his career as a New York surgeon—and he was only in his thirties. In September of that same year, Carl Koller announced at a medical congress in Heidelberg, Germany, that cocaine could be used as a local anesthetic. Hearing this, Halsted began experiments on himself. He found that if cocaine was injected into the trunk of a sensory nerve, all of its branches were numbed to pain, so he kept injecting larger amounts into himself and discovered that a larger area of the body could be numbed to pain.

He soon recognized that the more cocaine he injected into his body, the better he felt. In fact, he'd never felt better in his life: all his doubts and cares disappeared; unwittingly, he became addicted to cocaine. In a few short months, his personality changed noticeably. He neglected his work, was bored with his friends, and wanted to be alone most of the time. His ability to do surgery deteriorated steadily. His fellow surgeons were getting concerned about the harm he might do to his patients and himself, so they insisted that he be hospitalized in the Butler Hospital, in Providence, Rhode Island, for three months in late 1886.

Halsted agreed, but as soon as he was released from the hospital, he went back to injecting himself with cocaine, so, early in 1887, they forced him back to Butler Hospital, this time for six months. Again it didn't cure him, so they literally kicked him out of New York City, and told him to never come back.

Halsted moved to Baltimore, Maryland, where he appealed to his old friend, Dr. William H. Walsh, professor of pathology at Johns Hopkins University, to help him get rid of the onerous habit. I've combed many encyclopedias and studied reports from other sources for details of what came next; the consensus points to the following:

Halsted was put on a small ship and kept at sea for a year, guarded so closely that there was no way he could get cocaine surreptitiously. This cured him.

In 1889, he was appointed acting surgeon at the newly

opened Johns Hopkins Hospital. The appointment was for only one year, because of concerns about his past drug use. During this year he was frequently and without prior notice tested for cocaine use. Never was any found, so, in 1890, he was appointed surgeon-in-chief to the hospital, and in 1892 was promoted to professor of surgery. Thus he was the founding professor of surgery at Johns Hopkins Medical School, which opened in 1893. He retained these posts for the rest of his life.

During his time at Johns Hopkins, Halsted made many contributions to surgery, for which he is famous. He developed an organized system of training surgeons in a residency at the hospital. A "resident" is a young physician who has completed one year of internship, and then stays in the hospital four to seven years longer to become a specialist in the field he had chosen—in this case, surgery.

It's interesting to note that seven of Halsted's first ten residents became professors of surgery at various medical schools, which clearly demonstrates what a great teacher of surgery he was. He stressed to his residents gentle handling to avoid tissue destruction, careful hemostasis (stopping the flow of blood) to prevent subcutaneous blood clots, and layer-to-layer wound closures to avoid dead space. He was truly the originator of modern surgical practice.

Halsted discovered numerous new surgical techniques. He was one of the first to tackle surgical removal of aneurysms, and to repair hernias of the groin so that they never returned. He was one of the first to remove goiter tumors from the thyroid gland, and is famous for developing techniques of radical mastectomy for terminal breast cancer that saved many women from early death. Today of course, radical mastectomy has been replaced by modified mastectomy, radiation, and chemotherapy.

In 1889 Halsted's head nurse complained about the dermatitis she suffered as a result of mercuric chloride, the antiseptic they all had to use to wash their hands before surgery. All operations at that time were performed barehanded. Halsted contacted the Goodyear Rubber Company and asked it they could make thin rubber gloves for use by the surgery staff; Goodyear complied.

In June 1890 he married this same head nurse, Caroline Hampton. They had no children. Following their marriage, Halsted retired to his estate, Hugh Hampton, in Casheer's Valley, North Carolina, but only for a portion of each summer; otherwise he continued as a surgeon.

In 1919 Halsted became jaundiced from a stone in his bile duct. His gall bladder was full of stones and was removed, along with the stone in the bile duct. In 1922 he had a recurrence of jaundice that required an operation; he died on September 7, 1922, just one day afterward. He was seventy years old.

Epilogue

In closing, I want to repeat, "Life is a gift." We don't know how or why we were given life on this earth, nor do we know where we're going when our lives disappear. We're told that the universe has no boundaries; its stars are too numerous to count, and their distance from Earth is trillions and trillions of miles. When we look up into the sky at night, we can't help marveling at its beauty. The astronomers tell us the universe is still expanding, and no one knows its limits—facts that are incomprehensible to us.

But that really makes no difference. What's important is that we be impressed by the *intelligence* that created all this. If not *intelligence,* could the universe possibly have come about from an unfathomable bang, as some now claim, but can't explain where such power came from? So, if it's not a super power, a spirit, a human being, or something most call God, then who can deny that it must have been created by a master *intelligence*?

Therefore, there must be a reason for us to have been put on Earth. We must be a part of some super-plan of this master *intelligence.* It behooves us to do the best we can on Earth, so that when our time comes to die, we can be allowed to fit into the eternal puzzle.